David Mamet
Plays: 1

Duck Variations, Sexual Perversity in Chicago, Squirrels, American Buffalo, The Water Engine, Mr Happiness

Duck Variations: 'There is a marvellous ring of truth in the meandering, speculative talk of these old men. There is more here than just geriatric humour; there is also imagination and understanding . . . Mamet is a true and original writer, who cherishes words and, on the evidence at hand, cherishes characters even more.' *New Yorker*

Sexual Perversity in Chicago: 'Mamet is not so interested in what brings people together as he is in what keeps them apart . . . This is a compassionate, rueful comedy about how difficult it is, in our fucked-up society, for men to give themselves to women and for women to give themselves to men.' *Village Voice*

Squirrels: 'Memorably captures the agony of the creative process . . . and as in all Mamet's plays, there are gripping riffs of edgy, sawn-off dialogue, which compellingly chart the shifting balance of power between his characters.' *Daily Telegraph*

American Buffalo: 'There is nothing parodistic in Mamet's intentions, which aim to reveal character through language; or in his structure, which surges forward with the dense assuredness of a poem; or in his ear, which is tuned with transcriptive accuracy to the linguistic fall-out from generations of immigrant handling of the American tongue . . . This play is a parable about the US – not in the journalistic way of British state-of-the-nation dramas, but quietly, stealthily, with all the rich interior organisation of a true work of art.' *Observer*

The Water Engine is 'an American fable about "the common person and the institution" . . . The bare bones of the tale do no justice to the play's theatrical adroitness or the suggestive ambivalence of its tone . . . The great appeal of his work lies in his unerring ear for dialogue. His plays are full of theatrical opportunities. No matter how slight the scene, there is an unmistakable tension in the exchanges between the characters which brings them alive.' *Spectator*

Mr Happiness is a short ironic monologue, written as a complementary piece for the Broadway opening of *The Water Engine* in 1978.

David Mamet was born in Chicago in 1947. He studied at Goddard College, Vermont (where he was later Artist-in-Residence), and at the Neighborhood Playhouse School of Theater in New York. His first and many subsequent plays were first performed by the St Nicholas Theater Company, Chicago, of which he was a founding member and Artistic Director. In 1978 he became Associate Artistic Director of the Goodman Theater, Chicago, where *American Buffalo* had been first staged in 1975, subsequently winning an Obie Award and opening on Broadway in 1977 and at the National Theatre, London in 1978. *Sexual Perversity in Chicago* and *Duck Variations* (Regent Theatre, 1977), *A Life In The Theatre* (Open Space, 1979), *Glengarry Glen Ross* (National Theatre, 1983; Pulitzer Prize for Drama 1984), *Edmond* (Royal Court, 1985), *Oleanna* (Royal Court and Duke of York's Theatre, 1993) and *The Cryptogram* (Ambassadors Theatre, 1994) hav[...] Other plays include *Reunion, The Woods, The Wat[...] Lakeboat* (1982) and *The Disappearance of the Jews* [...] screenplays for *The Postman Always Rings Twice, T[...] Untouchables, Things Change* (written with Shel Silv[...] *No Angels, Hoffa, The Deer Slayer, High and Low* and [...]

DAVID MAMET

Plays: 1

Duck Variations
Sexual Perversity in Chicago
Squirrels
American Buffalo
The Water Engine
Mr Happiness

Methuen Drama

METHUEN DRAMA CONTEMPORARY DRAMATISTS

This collection first published in Great Britain in 1994 by Methuen Drama
and reissued in this series in 1996

20 19 18 17 16 15 14 13 12 11

Methuen Drama
A & C Black Publishers Ltd
38 Soho Square, London W1D 3HB

A CIP catalogue record for this book is available from the British Library

Duck Variations first published in Britain by Eyre Methuen in 1978,
copyright © 1971 by David Mamet
Sexual Perversity in Chicago first published in Britain by Eyre Methuen in 1978,
copyright © 1974 by David Mamet
Squirrels first published in Britain in this collection by Methuen Drama in 1994,
copyright © 1974 (under the title *The Bitten Hand*), 1982 by David Mamet
American Buffalo first published in Britain by Eyre Methuen in 1978,
copyright © 1975, 1976, 1978 by David Mamet
The Water Engine first published in Britain in this collection by Methuen Drama in 1994,
copyright © 1977, 1983 by David Mamet
Mr Happiness first published in Britain in this collection by Methuen Drama in 1994,
copyright © 1978 by David Mamet
This collection copyright © 1994 by Methuen Drama

The author has asserted his moral rights

ISBN 9-780413-645906

Typeset by Wilmaset, Birkenhead, Wirral
Printed and bound in Great Britain by Cox & Wyman Ltd, Reading, Berkshire

Caution

Contents

David Mamet:
A Chronology

PLAYS	USA	UK
Duck Variations, St Nicholas Theater Company, Chicago, 1972; Regent Theatre, London, 1977	1972	1977
Sexual Perversity in Chicago, Organic Theater Co., Chicago, 1974; Regent Theatre, London, 1977	1974	1977
Squirrels, St Nicholas Theater Company, Chicago, 1974; King's Head Theatre, London, 1993	1974	1993
American Buffalo, Goodman Theater Company, Chicago, 1975; National Theatre, London, 1978	1975	1978
Reunion, St Nicholas Theater Company, Chicago, 1976	1976	
The Woods, St Nicholas Theater Company, Chicago, 1977	1977	
The Water Engine, St Nicholas Theater Company, Chicago, 1977; Hampstead Theatre, London, 1989	1977	1989
A Life in the Theatre, Goodman Theater, Chicago; Theatre de Lys, New York, 1977; Brighton, 1989	1977	1989
Mr Happiness, New York Shakespeare Festival, New York, 1978	1978	
Prairie du Chien, National Public Radio, 1979; Royal Court Theatre Upstairs, London, 1986	1979	1986
Lakeboat, Court Street Theater, Milwaukee Rep, Milwaukee, WI, 1980	1980	
Edmond, Goodman Theater, Chicago, 1982; Royal Court Theatre, London, 1985	1982	1985
The Disappearance of the Jews, Goodman Theater, Chicago, 1983	1983	
Glengarry Glen Ross, Goodman Theater, Chicago, 1984; National Theatre, London, 1983	1984	1983

SCREENPLAYS

Duck Variations

The Characters:
Emil Varec and **George S Aronovitz** *Two gentlemen in their sixties*

The Scene:
A park on the edge of a big city on a lake.
An afternoon around Easter.

This is a very simple play.
The set should consist only of a park bench and perhaps a wire garbage can.
The actors can be discovered seated on the bench at rise, or they can come on together, or separately and meet.
Any blocking or business is at the discretion of individual actors and directors. There should be, though, an interval between each variation – it doesn't need to be a long one – to allow the actors to rest and prepare for the new variation. This interval is analogous to the space between movements in a musical presentation.

The Duck Variations was first produced by The St. Nicholas Theatre Company, at Goddard College, Plainfield, Vermont, in 1972, with the following cast:

Emil Varec	Pablo Vela
George S Aronovitz	Peter Vincent

Directed by David Mamet

It was first produced off-off Broadway at St. Clement's Theatre, New York City, in 1975, with the following cast:

Emil Varec	Paul Sparer
George S Aronovitz	Michael Egan

Directed by Albert Takazauckas

It was produced off-Broadway at the Cherry Lane Theatre, New York City, with *Sexual Perversity in Chicago*, in June 1976, with the following cast:

Emil Varec	Mike Kellin
George S Aronovitz	Michael Egan

Directed by Albert Takazauckas

As *Duck Variations*, the play's British première was at the Regent Theatre, London, in December 1977, with the following cast:

Emil Varec	Bernard Spear
George S Aronovitz	Gordon Sterne

Directed by Albert Takazauckas

FIRST VARIATION
It's nice, the park is nice

Emil It's nice.

George The park is nice.

Emil You forget.

George . . . you remember.

Emil I don't know . . .

George What's to know? There's a boat!

Emil So early?

George I suppose so . . . because there it is.

Emil I wonder if it's cold out there.

George There, here, it's like it is today. How it is *today*, that's how it is.

Emil But the boat is moving . . .

George So it's colder in relation how fast the boat is going.

Emil The water is colder than the land.

George So it's cold in relation to the water.

Emil So it's a different temperature on the boat than on a bench.

George They probably got sweaters.

Emil There's more than one in the boat?

George Wait till they come round again.

Emil Where did they go?

George Over there, behind the pier, where could they go?

Emil Not far . . . it's expensive a boat.

George They care?

Emil No.

George If they got the money for a *boat*, they can afford it.

Emil It's not cheap.

George I said it was cheap?

Emil Even a small boat.

George I know it's not cheap.

Emil Even a very small boat is expensive.

George Many times a small boat is even *more* expensive.

Emil Ah.

George Depending . . .

Emil Mmm.

George On many factors.

Emil Mmm.

George . . . the size of the boat . . .

Emil Yes.

George . . . the engine.

Emil Yes. The *size* of the engine.

George Certainly, certainly.

Emil The speed of the engine.

George Many factors.

Emil The speed of the *boat*.

George That. None of it's cheap. It's all very intricate.

Emil Cars.

George Boats, cars . . . air travel. The military. It was never cheap.

Emil Housing.

George (*looks*) There's two of them in the boat.

Emil It's the same boat?

George How many boats have we seen today?

Emil That's what I'm asking.

George One.

Emil (*looks*) Another boat!

George One, two . . .

Emil A real clipper, too.

George Where?

Emil Look at *her* will ya!

George That?

Emil What else? Go, sister!

George That?

Emil Sure as shootin'.

George That's the water pump.

Emil That?

George Yes.

Emil That?

George Yes.

Emil The pump house?

George Yes.

Emil She's the water pump?

George Yes.

Emil . . . look at her float.

George Mmm.

Emil Look at her . . . just sit there.

George Mmm.

Emil All year 'round.

George I'll give you that.

Emil What a life.

George Ducks!

Emil Where?

George Where I'm pointing.

Emil Ahh.

George A sure sign of spring.

Emil Autumn, too.

George Uh huh.

Emil . . . you see them . . .

George Yes.

Emil They go south . . .

George Um.

Emil They come back . . .

George Ummm.

Emil They live . . .

George They go . . .

Emil Ahhh.

George Ducks like to go . . .

Emil . . . yes?

George Where it's *nice* . . .

Emil Ehhh?

George *At that time*!

Emil Of course.

George And they're made so they just go. Something inside says it's getting a little cold . . . a little too cold . . .

Emil Like humans, they don't like cold.

George And there they go.

Emil There they go.

George And the same when it's warm.

Emil They come back.

George They got a leader. A lead duck. He starts . . . he's a duck. But he stays with the pack. Many times. He comes, he goes. He learns the route. Maybe he's got a little more on the ball.

Emil All this time there is another lead duck.

George Of course. But *he*, he goes, he lives, maybe he finds a mate . . .

Emil Yes.

George And he *waits* . . . The *lead* duck . . . who knows?

Emil He dies.

George One day, yes. He dies. He gets lost . . .

Emil And our duck moves up.

George *He* is now the leader. It is *he* who guides them from one home to the next. They all know the way. Each of them has it in him to know when the time is to move . . . But *he* . . . He will be in charge until . . .

Emil Yes.

George Just like the other one . . .

Emil There's no shame in that.

George Just like the previous duck . . .

Emil It happened to *him*, it's got to happen to *him*.

George The time comes to step down.

Emil He dies.

George He dies, he leaves . . . something. And another duck moves on up.

Emil And *someday*.

George Yes.

Emil Someone will take *his* place.

George Until . . .

Emil It's boring just to think about it.

SECOND VARIATION
The duck's life

George You know, the duck's life is not all hearts and flowers. He's got his worries, too. He's got fleas and lice and diseases of the body. Delusions. Wing problems. Sexual difficulties. Many things.

Emil It's not an easy life.

George Only the beginning. The duck is at the mercy of any elements in the vicinity. Sunspots. Miscarriage. Inappropriate changes in the weather.

Emil Yes.

George Hunters. Blight. Tornadoes. Traps. Any number of airplanes.

Emil Small vicious children.

George Chainstores. And, of course, the Blue Heron.

Emil Blue Heron?

George The hereditary Enemy of the Duck.

Emil Yeah?

George It's what they call symbiosis. They both live to insure the happiness of each other. The Blue Herons eat ducks, and the duck . . .

Emil Yes?

George The duck's part of the bargain . . .

Emil Is to be eaten by the Heron?

George Is to . . . Well it slips me for the moment, but it's not as one-sided as it might appear. Nature has given the duck speed and endurance and the art of concealment. She has made the Heron large and unwieldy and *blue* to be able to spot at a distance. On the other hand he has the benefits of size and occasional camouflage should he come up against something blue.

Emil And shaped like a bird.

George Not always necessary. The battle between the two is as old as time. The ducks propagating, the Herons eating them. The Herons multiplying and losing great numbers to exhaustion in the never-ending chase of the duck. Each keeping the other in check, down through history, until a bond of unspoken friendship and respect unites them, even in the embrace of death.

Emil So why do they continue to fight?

George Survival of the fittest. The never-ending struggle between heredity and environment. The urge to combat. Old as the oceans. Instilled in us all: Who can say to what purpose?

Emil Who?

George We do not know. But this much we *do* know. As long as the duck exists, he will battle day and night, sick and well with the Heron, for so is it writ. And as long as the sky is made dark with the wing of the Monster Bird, the Heron will feast on duck.

THIRD VARIATION
Also they got barnyard ducks

Emil Also they got barnyard ducks.

George Yeah. I know.

Emil That they raise for Easter and Thanksgiving.

George You're thinking of Turkeys.

Emil Also ducks.

George They keep 'em? In captivity?

Emil Yeah. In the Barnyard. They clip their wings.

George Uh.

Emil Yeah. What? You can't put 'em on their honour?!

George Times have changed.

Emil Vandalism . . . they fat 'em up. They feed 'em, the farmers, on special mixtures. Corn, and maybe an oat. And they got special injections they give 'em. To keep 'em happy.

George And they can't fly.

Emil No.

George All with wildness is gone.

Emil Just walking around the farm all day. Eating.

George They're allowed to mate?

Emil This we do not know.

George Eh?

Emil Only a few farmers know this.

George Yeah?

Emil The mating of ducks is a private matter between the duck in question and his mate.

George Yeah?

Emil It is a thing which few White men have witnessed . . . And those who claim to have seen it . . . strangely do not wish to speak.

George There are things we're better off not to know.

Emil If you don't know, you never can be forced to tell.

George They don't got those beaks for nothing.

Emil *Nothing* is for Nothing.

George Too true.

Emil Everything has got a purpose.

George True . . .

Emil Every blessed thing . . .

George Oh yes.

Emil . . . that lives has got a purpose.

George Ducks . . .

Emil Sweat glands . . .

George Yeah.

Emil We don't sweat for nothing, you know.

George I know it.

Emil Everything that lives must sweat.

George It's all got a purpose.

Emil It's all got a rhyme *and* a reason.

George The purpose of sweat is, in itself, not clear.

Emil Yes . . .

George But . . . there it is.

Emil A purpose and a reason. Even those we, at this time, do not clearly understand.

George Sure as shootin'.

Emil The yearly migration of the duck, to mate and take a little rest . . .

George Purpose.

Emil Sweat . . .

George Purpose.

Emil There's nothing you could possibly name that doesn't have a purpose. Don't even bother to try. Don't waste your time.

George I'm in no hurry.

Emil It's all got a purpose. The very fact that you are sitting here right now on this bench has got a purpose.

George And so, by process of elimination, does the bench.

Emil Now you're talking sense.

George Darn Tootin'.

Emil The law of the universe is a law unto itself.

George Yes. Yes.

Emil And woe be to the man who fools around.

George You can't get away with *nothing*.

Emil And if you *could* it would have a purpose.

George Nobody knows that better than me.

Emil . . . Well put.

FOURTH VARIATION
The duck is not like us

Emil The duck is not like us, you know.

George How so?

Emil The duck is an egg-bearing creature.

George And we're not, I suppose?

Emil I didn't say that. The young of the duck at birth are already trained to do things most humans learn only much later. Swim. Follow their mother.

George Fly.

Emil No. I don't believe they can fly until later life.

George But it's possible.

Emil It's possible, but you're wrong.

George . . . As a matter of fact I do remember reading somewhere that many small ducks *do* possess the ability to fly at birth.

Emil I do think you are mistaken.

George No. It could be . . . But no.

Emil Yes. I believe you're sadly wrong.

George No. I wouldn't *swear* to it . . .

Emil No.

George But I'd almost *swear* I've read that *somewhere* . . .

Emil Yes, I'm fairly sure you're wrong on that one point.

George Some little-known group of ducks.

Emil No. All my knowledge of nature tells me I must say no.

George A very small group of ducks.

Emil I cannot let that by.

George But I think . . .

Emil It's possible you *misread* the . . .

George Possibly, but . . .

Emil No, no. No. I must still stick to my saying no. No.

George . . . Perhaps I misread it. What a thing, however. To be able to fly. In later life.

Emil Swimming ain't so bad either.

George But any fool who knows how to swim can swim. It takes a *bird* to Fly.

Emil Insects also fly.

George But not in the same category.

Emil Insects . . . birds and insects and . . . I *could* be wrong but . . .

George You *are* wrong. Nothing else flies.

FIFTH VARIATION
Did you know what I was reading?

George Did you know what I was reading somewhere?

Emil Don't start.

George About the stratosphere. The stratosphere, particularly the lower stratosphere, is becoming messy with gook.

Emil Eh?

George According to the weatherman.

Emil *Our* stratosphere?

George Everybody's. Because it's all the same thing.

Emil Eh?

George As if you drop a pebble in a pond and the ripples spread you-know-not-where . . .

Emil Yes?

George So, when you stick shit up in the Stratosphere . . .

Emil Yes?

George You got the same problem.

Emil What kind of gook?

George All kinds. Dirt . . .

Emil Yes.

George Gook . . .

Emil No good.

George Automotive . . .

Emil Yeah.

George Cigarette smoke. It's all up there. It's not going anywhere.

Emil Yeah.

George They're finding out many things about the world we live in from the air.

Emil Yes.

George For, in many ways . . . the air is more a part of our world than we would like to admit. Think about it.

Emil I will.

George Planes that come down, they got to wash 'em right away. They go up clean, they come down filthy.

Emil Yes.

George But the creatures with no choice: Insects, ducks.

Emil Gliders.

George It's a shame. They should be shot.

Emil Some of them are shot.

George No, *them*, the ones responsible. Ducks! They're finding ducks with lung cancer. I was reading about this hunter in the forest and he shot a bunch of ducks that were laying down . . .

Emil Yes.

George And he missed. *But!* As he was walking away he heard this hacking, and he went back to investigate. And there were these five or six stunted ducks sitting in a clearing, hacking their guts out.

Emil No!

George Coughing and sneezing. Runny noses . . . and they'd flap their wings and go maybe two flaps and fall down coughing.

Emil It's no good for you.

George And he says instead of running off they came up and huddled around his feet with these rheumy, runny eyes. Looking quite pathetic. And he says he couldn't get it out of his mind . . .

Emil What?

George I'd feel silly to say it.

Emil Tell me.

George That they looked like they were trying to bum a smoke.

Emil . . . That's ridiculous.

George I know it.

Emil I think someone is putting you on.

George Very likely.

Emil You aren't even *supposed* to smoke in a forest.

George Go fight City Hall.

SIXTH VARIATION
What kind of a world is it?

George What kind of a world is it that can't even keep its streets clean?

Emil A self-destructive world.

George You said it.

Emil A cruel world.

George A dirty world. Feh. I'm getting old.

Emil Nobody's getting any younger.

George Almost makes a feller want to stop trying.

Emil Stop trying what?

George You know, life is a lot simpler than many people would like us to believe.

Emil How so?

George Take the duck.

Emil All right.

George Of what does his life consist?

Emil Well, flying . . .

George Yes.

Emil Eating.

George Yes.

Emil Sleeping.

George Yes.

Emil Washing himself

George Yes.

Emil Mating.

George Yes.

Emil And perhaps getting himself shot by some jerk in a red hat.

George Or 'Death.'

Emil Should we include that as one of the activities of life?

George Well, you can't die in a vacuum.

Emil That's true.

George So there we have it: the duck, too, is doomed to death . . .

Emil As are we all.

George But his life prior to that point is so much more simple. He is born. He learns his trade: to fly. He flies, he eats, he finds a mate, he has young, he flies some more, he dies. A simple, straight-forward easy-to-handle life.

Emil So what's your point?

George Well, lookit:

Emil Okay.

George On his deathbed what does the duck say if only he could speak?

Emil He wants to live some more.

George Right. But remorse? Guilt? Other bad feelings? No. No. He is in tune with nature.

Emil He is part of nature. He is a duck.

George Yes, but so is man a part of nature.

Emil Speak for yourself.

George I am speaking for myself.

Emil Then speak to yourself.

George Who asked you to listen?

Emil Who asked you to talk?

George Why are you getting upset?

Emil You upset me.

George Yeah?

Emil With your talk of nature and the duck and death. Morbid useless talk. You know, it is a good thing to be perceptive, but you shouldn't let it get in the way.

George And that is the point I was trying to make.

SEVENTH VARIATION
Yes, in many ways

George Yes, in many ways Nature is our window to the world.

Emil Nature *is* the world.

George Which shows you how easy it is to take a good idea and glop it up.

Emil So who do you complain to.

George Well, you complain to me.

Emil Do you mind?

George I'm glad I got the time to listen.

Emil A man needs a friend in this life.

George In this or any other life.

Emil You said it. Without a friend, life is not . . .

George Worth living?

Emil No it's still worth living. I mean, what is worth living if not life? No. But life without a friend is . . .

George It's lonely.

Emil It sure is. You said it. It's good to have a friend.

George It's good to be a friend.

Emil It's good to have a friend to talk to.

George It's good to talk to a friend.

Emil To complain to a friend . . .

George It's good to listen . . .

Emil Is good.

George To a friend.

Emil To make life a little less full of pain . . .

George I'd try anything.

Emil Is good.

George For you, or for a friend. Because it's good to help.

Emil To help a friend in need is the most that any man can want to do.

George And you couldn't ask for more than that.

Emil I wouldn't.

George Good.

Emil Being a loner in this world . . .

George Is not my bag of tea.

Emil Is no good. No man is an Island to himself.

George Or to anyone else.

Emil You can't live alone forever. You can't live forever anyway. But you can't live alone. Nothing that lives can live alone. Flowers. You never find just one flower. Trees. Ducks.

George Cactus.

Emil Lives alone?

George Well, you take the cactus in the waste. It stands alone as far as the eye can tell.

Emil But there are other cacti.

George Not in that immediate area, no.

Emil What are you trying to say?

George That the *cactus*, unlike everything else that cannot live alone, *thrives* . . .

Emil I don't want to hear it.

George But it's true, the cactus.

Emil I don't want to hear it. If it's false, don't waste my time and if it is true I don't want to know.

George It's a proven fact.

Emil I can't hear you.

George Even the duck sometimes.

Emil (*looks*) . . . Nothing that lives can live alone.

EIGHTH VARIATION
Ahh, I don't know

Emil Ahh, I don't know.

George So what?

Emil You gotta point . . . Sometimes I think the park is more trouble than it's worth.

George How so?

Emil To come and look at the lake and the trees and animals and sun just once in a while and traipse back. Back to . . .

George Your apartment.

Emil Joyless. Cold concrete. Apartment. Stuff. Linoleum. Imitation.

George The park is more real?

Emil The Park? Yes.

George Sitting on benches.

Emil Yes.

George Visiting tame animals?

Emil Taken from wildest captivity.

George Watching a lake that's a sewer?

Emil At least it's water.

George You wanna drink it?

Emil I drink it every day.

George Yeah. After it's been pured and filtered.

Emil A lake just the same. My inland sea.

George Fulla inland shit.

Emil It's better than nothing. Well, it's a close second.

George But why does it hurt you to come to the park?

Emil I sit home, I can come to the park. At the park the only place I have to go is home.

George Better not to have a park?

Emil I don't know.

George Better not to have a Zoo? We should forget what a turtle is?

Emil Aaaaah.

George Our children should never know the joy of watching some animal . . . behaving?

Emil I don't know.

George They should stay home and know only guppies eating their young.

Emil
Let 'em go to the country.
Nature's playground.
The country.
The land that time forgot.
Mallards in formation.
Individual barnyard noises.
Horses.
Rusty gates.
An ancient tractor.
Hay, barley.
Mushrooms.
Rye.
Stuffed full of abundance.
Enough to feed the nations of the
World.

George We'll have 'em over. We don't get enough riff-raff.

Emil Enough to gorge the countless cows of South America.

George Did you make that up?

Emil Yes.

George I take my hat off to you.

Emil Thank you.

George 'Feed the many' . . . how does it go?

Emil Um. Stuff the nameless . . . It'll come to me.

George When you get it, tell me.

NINTH VARIATION
At the Zoo they got ducks

Emil At the Zoo they got ducks. They got. What do you call it? . . . A Mallard. They got a mallard and a . . . what is it? A cantaloupe.

George You mean an antelope.

Emil No . . . no, it's not cantaloupe. But it's *like* cantaloupe. Uh . . .

George Antelope?

Emil No! *Antelope* is like an elk. What *I'm* thinking is like a duck.

George Goose?

Emil No. But it's . . . What sounds like *cantaloupe*, but it isn't.

George . . . Antelope. I'm sorry, but that's it.

Emil No. Wait! Wait. Ca . . . cala . . . camma . . . grantal . . .

George Canadian ducks?

Emil No! I've *seen* 'em, the ones I mean. I've seen 'em in the Zoo.

George Ducks?

Emil Yes! Ducks that I'm talking about. By God, I know what I mean . . . They're called . . . The only thing that comes up is canta. Pantel. Pandel. Panda . . . Candarolpe . . .

George They ain't got no panda.

Emil I know it . . . Panna . . .

George They *had* a panda at the *other* Zoo but it died.

Emil Yeah. Nanna . . .

George There were two of 'em. Or three. But they were all men and when they died . . . they couldn't have any babies, of course . . .

Emil Randspan?

George . . . so the Pandas . . .

Emil . . . lope . . .

George Died.

Emil Lo . . . lopa? Loola . . .

George Not Swans?

Emil No. Please. I know Swans. I'm talking about ducks.

George I know it.

Emil Can . . .

George Those Pandas were something.

Emil Yeah.

George Giant Pandas.

Emil Yeah.

George *Big* things.

Emil I've seen 'em.

George Not lately you haven't.

Emil No.

George Cause they been dead.

Emil I know it.

George From the Orient. Pandas from the Far East. There for all to see.

Emil Mantalope?

George Black and White.

Emil Palapope . . .

George Together.

Emil Maaaa . . .

George The Giant Panda.

Emil Fanna . . .

George Over two stories tall.

Emil Raaa?

George It got too expensive to feed it. They had to put 'em to sleep.

TENTH VARIATION
It's a crying shame

Emil It's a crying shame.

George Eh?

Emil A crying piss-laden shame. A blot on our time. Gook on the scutcheon. Oil slicks from here to Africa.

George Huh?

Emil They don't allow no smoking on ocean liners. One spark overboard and the whole ocean goes.

George Yeah?

Emil Oil-bearing ducks floating up dead on the beaches. Beaches closing. No place to swim. The surface of the sea is solid dying wildlife. In Australia . . . they're finding fish, they're going blind from lack of sun. New scary species are developing. They eat nothing but dead birds.

George Yeah?

Emil Catfish.

George . . . I think that's something different.

Emil Nevermore. Thrushes. No more the duck. Blue-jays. Cardinals. Making the dead ocean their last home.

George When I was young . . .

Emil Floating up dead on the beaches.

George Around my house . . .

Emil Their lungs a sodden pulp of gasoline. They're made for something better than that.

George In the springtime we used to . . .

Emil Can't even burn leaves in the fall. We have to wrap them in Plastic. Next we'll have to wrap each leaf individually. Little envelopes for each leaf, it shouldn't contaminate us with the vapours. Little numbered packets.

George Our lawn was.

Emil What?

George Eh?

Emil What was your lawn?

George I forget.

Emil Can you imagine, being the last man alive to have seen a blue heron? Or a wild buffalo?

George No man can live in the path of a wild buffalo.

Emil All right. A regular buffalo, then.

George They got 'em at the zoo.

Emil Buffaloes?

George Yeah, they got plenty of 'em.

Emil But that's in captivity.

George I should hope so.

Emil Well, in any case, you see my point.

George Yes . . .

Emil Well, that's the point I was trying to make.

ELEVENTH VARIATION
You know, I remember

George You know, I remember reading somewhere . . .

Emil Please.

George All right.

Emil I hurt your feelings.

George Yes.

Emil I'm sorry.

George I know.

Emil There is no excuse for that.

George It's all right.

Emil What were you gonna say?

George About the balance of nature.

Emil Yes?

George Being dependent on one of the Professional Spectator Sports.

Emil You're fulla shit.

George For its continuation.

Emil What made you think of that?

George I'm not sure.

Emil Some sport?

George I don't know.

Emil Nature?

George Perhaps.

Emil Do you remember which sport?

George I . . . no, I wouldn't want to go on record as remembering. One of the Major League sports.

Emil Where did you read it?

George I don't know. *The Readers' Digest* . . .

Emil Eh?

George Also they've found a use for cancer.

Emil Knock wood.

George It's about time. All the millions we spend on research, cigarettes . . .

Emil Wildlife.

George Nothing wrong with spending money on Wildlife.

Emil It's all take, take, take.

George Nature gives it back many times over.

Emil Yeah?

George A blue heron at sunset.

Emil They're all dead . . .

George A whiff of breeze from the lake . . .

Emil . . . or hiding.

George A flight of Ducks.

Emil The duck is, after all, only a bird.

George But what a bird.

Emil A pigeon, too, is a bird.

George There's no comparison.

Emil What is the difference between a duck and a pigeon?

George Basically, a lack of comparison.

Emil Aside from that?

George It is a difference of . . . self-respect. You can't argue with that.

Emil I won't begin.

George It wouldn't get you anywhere.

Emil Ha. Ha.

George Big talk.

Emil I'm ready to back it up.

George Oh yeah?

Emil Yeah.

George All right.

Emil . . . anytime you're ready.

George I'm ready.

Emil All right, then.

George Are you ready?

Emil You betcha, Red Ryder.

George Good.

Emil . . . Hey! What? Grownups squabbling about birds?

George You started it.

Emil I beg to differ.

George Go right ahead.

Emil All right, I *do* differ.

George It makes no difference. I was holding an intelligent conversation and then you came along . . .

Emil And simply pointed out that you were turning something into a thing which it is not.

George What is more noble than a duck.

Emil Depends on the duck.

George Is a pigeon more noble than a duck.

Emil Are you saying that just because the duck is wild and has no rules . . .

George No rules? No rules? No rules but the sun and the moon! No rules but the law of the seasons and when to go where at what specific time? No rules but to find a mate and cleave into her until death does him part?

Emil Is that true?

George It surely is.

Emil That I didn't know.

George Well, learn from your mistakes.

Emil I will.

George No rules!

Emil All right.

George One of the most rigid creatures.

Emil I'm sorry.

George Did you know that many human societies are modelled on those of our animal friends?

Emil Pish.

George I beg to differ about it.

Emil Pish foo.

George The French, for example.

Emil Are modelled on animals?

George Historically, yes.

Emil Where did you get that?

George Some guide to France.

Emil I don't believe it.

George I got it somewhere, I'll show you.

Emil You do that.

George I will.

Emil You just do that.

George Don't push me.

Emil I won't.

George All right.

Emil Darn tootin'.

TWELFTH VARIATION
Whenever I think of wild flying things

Emil Whenever I think of wild flying things I wonder.

George Yes?

Emil If, in the City, as we are . . .

George Yes?

Emil We maybe . . .

George Yes?

Emil Forget it.

George Ducks.

Emil Ducks.

George Ducks. Flying wild.

Emil Wild over boundaries.

George Lakes, rivers.

Emil Imaginary lines . . .

George The Equator.

Emil Never minding . . . Never stopping . . .

George Stopping for no man.

Emil High above unmanned terrain.

George Barren.

Emil Unexplored North Country.

George Naked. Strange.

Emil Here and there a Mountie.

George Cold.

Emil Nowhere to rest.

George What a life.

Emil Sleeping on the fly.

George Blown by storms.

Emil You know, that is not a laughing matter . . .

George Who's laughing?

Emil Much wildlife is, I am about to tell you, killed each year in storms and similar . . . things where they have a lot of wind.

George Don't I know it.

Emil Another countless danger for the duck.

George Frost, too.

Emil Hail.

George Uh.

Emil Can you imagine it?

George . . . Hail . . .

Emil Pelting the poor creature. Alone in the sky. Many feet in the air. He can't go right, he can't go left . . .

George Nowhere to go.

Emil Hail all over. Hitting him. Pelting him. Making ribbons of his wings. Creaming him out of the sky.

George The Law of Life.

Emil That's what you say *now*.

George Some must die so others can live.

Emil But they must die, too.

George So some must die so others can live a little longer. That's implied.

Emil And then *they* die.

George Of course. So that others can live. It makes sense if you think about it.

THIRTEENTH VARIATION
They stuff them.

Emil They stuff them.

George Eh?

Emil They stuff them. They shoot them and they stuff them.

George So long as they're dead.

Emil Sawdust. And they tack 'em on the wall.

George Also they stuff 'em for the oven.

Emil That too.

George Yeah.

Emil But to kill for no reason . . . without rhyme or reason . . . to shoot them. What a waste.

George Yes.

Emil What a waste in the life of a duck. To be shot. And not even eaten. Shot. Shot down like some animal.

George At least they shoot 'em in the air.

Emil Huh?

George Yeah! What do you think? You can't shoot 'em on foot? What!?

Emil Yeah?

George They got *laws*. Seasons. Didn't you ever hear of Duck Season?

Emil Of course.

George Well, duck season is when you can kill 'em. Legally.

Emil And when is it?

George Duck season?

Emil Yeah.

George Uh, the spring. Several weeks . . . The fall several weeks.

Emil . . . whenever the duck is *around*!

George No, it's . . .

Emil Eh?

George No, I . . .

Emil *Eh?*

George Well . . . ?

Emil *EH?*

George . . . yeah!

Emil They got the season so the only time it's not legal to shoot 'em is when they *ain't here*. . . . yeah.

Emil They're no dummies.

George Yeah.

Emil Influence . . . strings.

George It ain't cheap to hunt ducks.

Emil Are you kidding me?

George No. You need land.

Emil You need a *lot* of land.

George At least a mile. And you need . . .

Emil Guns.

George One gun only.

Emil And a spare.

George And some ammo to put *in* the gun.

Emil Telescope.

George And those hats.

Emil A blatter to call them.

George Not always necessary.

Emil But good to have in an emergency. . . . A bag to put them in.

George Big boots.

Emil A raincoat.

George A radio.

Emil You gotta take lunch.

George You need a lotta things.

Emil A licence.

George And a *lot* of luck.

Emil Oh, yes.

George It's easy to pick out a little wobbling duck from miles in a clear blue sky?

Emil No.

George A *LOT* of luck.

Emil And practice.

George Who's got the time?

Emil Every day. A half hour anyway. Practising . . .

George . . . is where they separate the men from the boys. At that moment there is no turning back. You're committed. You've been blatting around and searching the sky and crouching 'till your back hurts. From dawn on.

Emil Yes.

George Lying on the cold Earth, trying not to look like anything. Hoping. Praying for that ONE DUCK . . .

Emil A low flying duck . . .

George That one chance to show what *dreams* are made of. Until . . .

Emil Yes?

George Until . . . off in the distance. *Beyond* the horizon 'til you don't even know what it is, is a honking. The honking comes closer. Closer and louder. You see a far-off blur. The blur becomes a speck. The speck gets bigger. It's a big speck. It's a dot. The dot is advancing and it's honking and the honking is louder and becomes clear and precise. You can just make it out. Flapping. Flying straight in a line to join its comrades. Frantic. Lost. Dangerous. Vicious: A DUCK. . . . and on he comes. You quietly raise from the ground. One knee . . . two knees. You lift the gun, you put the gun on your shoulder and point it at the duck. It's you and him. You and the duck on the marsh. He wants to go home and you want to kill him for it. So you fire the gun. Once, again. Again. Again. Your ears are ringing. Your eyes are covered in spots. You cannot see. You are quivering and you gotta sit down. Your heart is going fast . . .

Emil Where's the duck?

George . . . slowly. Slowly you lower yourself to the Earth. Your joints creak . . .

Emil Where's the duck?

George . . . slowly. Slowly you lower yourself to the Earth. Your joints creak . . .

Emil *Where's the duck?*

George . . . with the weight of your body. Your shoulder aches from pounding, and your . . .

Emil *WHERE'S THE DUCK?*

George The duck is dying.

Emil Out in the marsh.

George Out in the marsh.

Emil Oh no.

George In a flock of feathers and blood. Full of bullets. Quiet, so as not to make a sound. Dying.

Emil Living his last.

George Dying.

Emil Leaving the Earth and sky.

George Dying.

Emil Lying on the ground.

George Dying.

Emil Fluttering.

George Dying.

Emil Sobbing.

George Dying.

Emil Quietly bleeding.

George Thinking.

Emil Dying.

George Dying, dying.

Emil But wait! This here! He summons his strength for one last time.

George No.

Emil Maybe he beats around and tries to make it . . .

George No.

Emil Back in the air?

George No.

Emil One last . . .

George No.

Emil A flutter of . . .

George No.

Emil A little . . .

George No.

Emil He's dead, isn't he?

George *nods.*

Emil I knew it.

George The Law of Life.

FOURTEENTH VARIATION
For centuries prior to this time

Emil You know, for centuries prior to this time man has watched birds.

George I still watch 'em.

Emil To obtain the secret of Flight.

George We're better off without it.

Emil Yeah.

George They'll go to their graves with it.

Emil The Ancient Greeks used to sit around all day looking at birds.

George Yeah?

Emil Oh yes. They'd take a chair and go sit and look at 'em. Just watch them all day long and wonder.

George I, too, would wonder. A crumbling civilization and they're out in the Park looking at birds.

Emil
There were the Ancient Greeks.
Old. Old men.
Incapable of working.
Of no use to their society.
Just used to watch the birds all day
First Light to Last Light.
First Light: Go watch birds.
Last Light: Stop watching birds. Go
Home.
Swallows. Falcons.
Forerunners of our modern birds.
And the forerunners of our modern
States.
Greeks. Birds.
Used to sit out all day long. Sit on a
bench and feed them . . .
Give them little bits of . . .

George . . . rice?

Emil Rice, yes. History is not completely clear on that point, but we can imagine rice. For the sake of argument. Rich, sleek birds of prey.

George And fat old men.

Emil
Watching each other.
Each with something to contribute.
That the world might turn another day.

A Fitting end.
To some very noble creatures of the
sky.
And a lotta Greeks.

Sexual Perversity in Chicago

The Characters:
Dan Shapiro, *an urban male in his late twenties*
Bernard Litko, *a friend and associate of Dan Shapiro*
Deborah Soloman, *a woman in her late twenties*
Joan Webber, *friend and room-mate of Deborah Soloman*

The Scene:
Various spots around the north side of Chicago, a big city on a lake.

The Time:
Approximately nine weeks one summer.

Sexual Perversity in Chicago was first produced by The Organic Theatre
Company, Chicago, Illinois, in the summer of 1974, with the following cast:

Bernard	Warren Casey
Dan	Eric Loeb
Deborah	Carolyn Gordon
Joan	Roberta Custer

Directed by Stuart Gordon

It was produced off-off Broadway at St. Clement's Theatre, New York
City, in December 1975, with the following cast:

Bernard	Robert Townsend
Dan	Robert Picardo
Deborah	Jane Anderson
Joan	Gina Rogers

Directed by Albert Takazauckas

It opened off-Broadway at the Cherry Lane Theatre, New York City, in
June 1976, produced by Larry Goossen and Jeffrey Wachtel, with the
following cast:

Bernard	F. Murray Abraham
Dan	Peter Riegert
Deborah	Jane Anderson
Joan	Gina Rogers

Directed by Albert Takazauckas

The play's British première was at the Regent Theatre, London, in
December 1977, with the following cast:

Bernard	Kenneth Nelson
Dan	Stephen Hoye
Deborah	Glory Annen
Joan	Gina Rogers

Directed by Albert Takazauckas

Note: Some portions of the dialogue appear in parentheses, which serve
to mark a slight change of outlook on the part of the speaker – perhaps a
momentary change to a more introspective regard. – D.M.

A singles bar. **Dan Shapiro** *and* **Bernard Litko** *are seated at the bar.*

Danny So how'd you do last night?

Bernie Are you kidding me?

Danny Yeah?

Bernie Are you fucking kidding me?

Danny Yeah?

Bernie Are you pulling my leg?

Danny So?

Bernie So tits out to here so.

Danny Yeah?

Bernie Twenty, a couple years old.

Danny You gotta be fooling.

Bernie Nope.

Danny You devil.

Bernie You think she hadn't been around?

Danny Yeah?

Bernie She hadn't gone the route?

Danny She knew the route, huh?

Bernie Are you fucking kidding me?

Danny Yeah?

Bernie She *wrote* the route.

Danny No shit, around twenty, huh?

Bernie Nineteen, twenty.

Danny You're talking about a girl.

Bernie Damn right.

Danny You're telling me about some underage stuff.

Bernie She don't gotta be but eighteen.

Danny Was she?

Bernie Shit yes.

Danny Then okay.

Bernie She made eighteen easy.

Danny Well, then.

Bernie Had to punch in at twenty, twenty-five easy.

Danny Then you got no problem.

Bernie I know I got no problem.

Danny So tell me.

Bernie So okay, so where am I?

Danny When?

Bernie Last night, two-thirty.

Danny So two-thirty, you're probably over at Yak-Zies.

Bernie Left Yak-Zies at one.

Danny So you're probably over at Grunts.

Bernie They only got a two o'clock licence.

Danny So you're probably over at the Commonwealth.

Bernie So okay, so I'm over at the Commonwealth, in the pancake house off the lobby, and I'm working on a stack of those raisin and nut jobs . . .

Danny They're good.

Bernie . . . and I'm reading the paper, and I'm reading, and I'm casing the pancake house, and the usual shot, am I right?

Danny Right.

Bernie So who walks in over to the cash register but this chick.

Danny Right.

Bernie Nineteen-, twenty-year-old chick . . .

Danny Who we're talking about.

Bernie . . . and she wants a pack of Viceroys.

Danny I can believe that.

Bernie Gets the smokes, and she does this number about how she forget her purse up in her room.

Danny Up in her room?

Bernie Yeah.

Danny Was she a pro?

Bernie At that age?

Danny Yeah.

Bernie Well, at this point we don't know. So anyway, I go over and ask her can I front her for the smokes, and she says she couldn't, and then she says Well, all right, and would I like to join her in a cup of coffee.

Danny She asked you . . .

Bernie . . . yeah.

Danny For a cup of coffee?

Bernie Right?

Danny And all this time she was nineteen?

Bernie Nineteen, twenty. So down we sit and get to talking. This, that, blah, blah, blah, and 'Come up to my room and I'll pay you back for the cigarettes.'

Danny No.

Bernie Yeah.

Danny You're shitting me.

Bernie I'm telling you.

Danny And was she a pro?

Bernie So at this point, we don't know. Pro, semi-pro, Betty Coed from College, regular young broad, it's anybody's ballgame. So, anyway, up we go. Fifth floor on the alley and it's 'Sit down, you wanna drink?' 'What you got?', 'Bourbon,' 'Fine.' And goddam if she doesn't lay half a rock on me for the cigarettes.

Danny No.

Bernie Yeah.

Danny So this changes the complexity of things.

Bernie For a bit, yes. But *then* what shot does she up and pull?

Danny You remind her of her ex.

Bernie No.

Danny She's never done anything like this before in her life?

Bernie No.

Danny She just got into town, and do you know where a girl like her could make a little money?

Bernie No.

Danny So I'm not going to lie to you, what shot does she pull?

Bernie The shot she is pulling is the following two things: (a) she says 'I think I want to take a shower.'

Danny No.

Bernie Yes. And (b) she says 'And then let's fuck.'

Danny Yeah?

Bernie What did I just tell you?

Danny She said that?

Bernie I hope to tell you.

Danny Nineteen years old?

Bernie Nineteen, twenty.

Danny And was she a pro?

Bernie So at this point I don't know. But I do say I'll join her in the shower, if she has no objections.

Danny Of course.

Bernie So into the old shower. And does this broad have a *body*?

Danny Yeah?

Bernie Are you kidding me?

Danny So tell me.

Bernie The *tits* . . .

Danny Yeah?

Bernie The *legs* . . .

Danny The ass?

Bernie Are you fucking fooling me? The *ass* on this broad . . .

Danny Young ass, huh?

Bernie Well yeah, young broad, young ass.

Danny Right.

Bernie And lathering her . . .

Danny Mmmm.

Bernie And drop the *soap* . . . This, that, and we get out. Towelling off, each of us in his or her full glory. So while we're towelling off, I flick the towel at her, very playfully, and by accident it catches her a good one on the ass, and *thwack*, a big red mark.

Danny No.

Bernie So I'm all sorry and so forth. But what does this broad do but let out a squeal of pleasure and relief that would fucking kill a horse.

Danny Huh?

Bernie So what the hell, I'm liberal.

Danny If that's her act, that's her act.

Bernie Goes without saying. So I look around, figuring to follow in my footsteps, and what is handy but this little G.E. clock radio. So I pick the mother up and heave it at her. Catches her across the shoulder blades, and we've got this long welt.

Danny Draw blood?

Bernie At this point, no. So what does she do? She says 'wait a minute,' and she crawls under the bed. From under the bed she pulls this suitcase, and from out of the suitcase comes this World War II Flak Suit.

Danny They're hard to find.

Bernie Zip, zip, zip, and she gets into the Flak Suit and we get down on the bed.

Danny What are you doing?

Bernie Fucking.

Danny She's in the Flak Suit?

Bernie Right.

Danny How do you get in?

Bernie How do you think I get in? She leaves the zipper open.

Danny That's what I thought.

Bernie But the shot is, while we're fucking, she wants me, every thirty seconds or so, to go BOOM at the top of my lungs.

Danny At her?

Bernie No, just in general. So we're humping and bumping and greasing the old Flak Suit and every once in a while I go BOOM, and she starts in on me. 'Turn me over,' she says, so I do. She's on her stomach. I'm on top . . .

Danny They got a flap in the back of the Flak Suit?

Bernie Yes. So she's on her stomach, *etcetera*. In the middle of everything she slithers over to the side of the bed, picks up the house phone and says, 'Give me Room 511.'

Danny Right.

Bernie 'Who are you calling?' I say. 'A friend,' she says. So okay. They answer the phone. 'Patrice,' she says, 'It's me, I'm up here with a friend, and I could use a little help. Could you help me out?'

Danny Ah ha!

Bernie So wait. So I don't know what the shot is. So all of a sudden I hear coming out of the phone: 'Rat Tat Tat Tat Tat. Ka POW! AK AK AK AK AK AK AK *Ka Pow!*' So fine. I'm pumping away, the chick on the other end is making airplane noises, every once in a while I go BOOM, and the broad on the bed starts going crazy. She's moaning and groaning and about to go the whole long route. Humping and bumping, and she's screaming 'Red dog One to Red dog Squadron' . . . all of a sudden she screams 'Wait.' She wriggles out, leans under the bed, and she pulls out this five-gallon jerrycan.

Danny Right.

Bernie Opens it up . . . it's full of gasoline. So she splashes the mother all over the walls, whips a fuckin'

Zippo out of the Flak suit, and WHOOSH, the whole
room is in flames. So the whole fuckin' joint is going up in
smoke, the telephone is going 'Rat Tat Tat,' the broad
jumps back on the bed and yells 'Now, give it to me *now*
for the love of Christ.' (*Pause.*) So I look at the broad . . .
and I figure . . . fuck this nonsense. I grab my clothes, I
peel a saw-buck off my wad, as I make the door I fling it
at her. 'For cab fare,' I yell. She doesn't hear nothing.
One, two, six, I'm in the hall. Struggling into my shorts
and hustling for the elevator. Whole fucking hall is full of
smoke, above the flames I just make out my broad, she's
singing 'Off we go into the Wild Blue Yonder,' and the
elevator arrives, and the whole fucking hall is full of
firemen. (*Pause.*) Those fucking firemen make out like
bandits. (*Pause.*)

Danny Nobody does it normally anymore.

Bernie It's these young broads. They don't know what
the fuck they want.

Danny You think she was a pro?

Bernie A pro, Dan . . .

Danny Yes.

Bernie . . . is how you think about yourself. You see my
point?

Danny Yeah.

Bernie Well, all right, then. I'll tell you one thing . . . she
knew all the pro moves.

Joan *and* **Deb** *at the apartment that they share.* **Joan** *is getting
ready to go out.*

Joan Men.

Deborah Yup.

Joan They're all after only one thing.

Deborah Yes. I know. (*Pause.*)

Joan But it's never the *same* thing.

Joan *is at a singles bar seated alone.* **Bernard** *spots her and moves to her table.*

Bernie Evening. Good evening.

Joan Good evening.

Bernie How would you like some company. (*Pause.*) What if I was to sit down here? What would that do for you, huh?

Joan No, I don't think so, no.

Pause.

Is there something I can do for you?

Bernie Nope. Not a thing in the world, no. I'm just *standing* here, looking for some place to sit down, huh? (*Pause.*)

Sits down at her table.

Well, is it a free country, or what?

Joan Don't torture me, just let me hear it, okay?

Bernie (*pause*) So here I am. I'm just in town for a one-day layover and I happen to find myself in this bar. So, so far so good. What am I going to do? I could lounge alone and lonely and stare into my drink, or I could take the bull by the horns and make an effort to enjoy myself . . .

Joan Are you making this up?

Bernie So hold on. So I see you seated at this table and I say to myself, 'Doug McKenzie, there is a young woman,' I say to myself, 'What is she doing here?', and I think she is here for the same reasons as I. To enjoy herself, and perhaps, to meet provocative people. (*Pause.*) I'm a meteorologist for TWA. It's an incredibly interesting, but

lonely job . . . Stuck in the cockpit of some jumbo jet
hours at a time . . . nothing to look at but charts . . .
What are you drinking?

Joan Scotch on the rocks.

Bernie You're a scotch drinker, huh?

Joan Yes.

Bernie Well, what the hell, you're drinking scotch. But I
say 'Why pigeonhole ourselves?' A person makes an effort
to enjoy himself, why pin a label on it, huh? This is life.
You learn a lot about life working for the airlines. Because
you're constantly in touch (you know with what?) with the
idea of Death. (*Pause.*) Not that I'm a fan of morbidness,
and so on. I mean. To meet interesting new people or not.
(*Pause.*) What else is there?

Joan Can I tell you something?

Bernie You bet.

Joan Forgive me if I'm being too personal . . . but I do
not find you sexually attractive. (*Pause.*)

Bernie What is that, some new kind of line? Huh? I
mean, not that I mind what you think, if that's what you
think . . . but . . . that's a fucking rotten thing to say.

Joan I'll live.

Bernie All kidding aside . . . lookit, I'm a fucking
professional, huh? My life is a bunch of having to make
split-second decisions. Life or death fucking decisions. So
that's what it is, so okay. I work hard, I play hard. Comes
I got a day off I wanna relax a bit . . . I wander – quite
by accident – into this bar. I have a drink or two . . .
perhaps a drop too much. Perhaps I get *too* loose (it's been
known to happen). So what do I see? A nice young
woman sitting by herself . . .

Joan We've done this one.

Bernie So just who the fuck do you think you are, God's gift to Women? I mean where do you fucking get off with this shit. You don't want to get come on to, go enroll in a convent. You think I don't have better things to do? I don't have better ways to spend my off hours than to listen to some nowhere cunt try out cute bits on me? I mean why don't you just clean your fucking act up, Missy. You're living in a city in 1976. (*Pause.*) Am I getting through to you?

Joan I think I'd like to be left alone.

Bernie Ah, you're breaking my heart. My fucking heart is pumping pisswater for you. You're torturing me with your pain and aloofness. You know that?

Joan I'm terribly sorry.

Bernie Sorry don't mean shit. You're a grown woman, behave like it for chrissakes. Huh? I mean, what the fuck do you think society is, just a bunch of rules strung together for your personal pleasure?

Joan Sometimes I think I'm not a very nice person.

Bernie You flatter yourself. (**Joan** *rises*.) So where are you going now?

Joan My little boy is sick, and I really should be getting home.

Bernie Cockteaser.

Joan I beg your pardon?

Bernie You heard me.

Joan I have never been called that in my life.

Bernie Well, you just lost your cherry.

Joan I . . . I find that very insulting.

Bernie Go get a lawyer, bitch. Go get a writ, you got yourself a case.

Pause.

Joan (*sits down again*) I . . . I'm . . . I'm sorry if I was being rude to you.

Bernie Oh, you're sorry if you were being rude to me.

Joan Yes.

Bernie You got a lot of fuckin' nerve. (*Rises, calls for check, goes.*)

At work. **Dan** *and* **Bernard** *are at work. They are filing.*

Bernie The main thing, Dan . . .

Danny Yes?

Bernie The main thing about *broads* . . .

Danny Yes?

Bernie Is two things. One: The Way to Get Laid is to Treat 'Em Like Shit . . .

Danny Yeah . . .

Bernie . . . and Two: Nothing . . . *nothing* makes you so attractive to the opposite sex as getting your rocks off on a regular basis.

The library. **Deb** *is seated, working.* **Dan** *cruises her and so on.*

Danny Hi.

Deborah Hello.

Danny I saw you at the Art Institute.

Deborah Uh huh.

Danny I remembered your hair.

Deborah Hair memory.

Danny You were in the Impressionists room. (*Pause.*) *Monet* . . . (*Pause.*)

Deborah Uh huh.

Danny You're very attractive. I like the way you look. (*Pause.*) You were drawing in charcoal. It was nice. (*Pause.*) Are you a student at the Art Institute?

Deborah No, I work.

Danny Work, huh? . . . work. (*Pause.*) I'll bet you're good at it. (*Pause.*) Is someone taking up a lot of your time these days?

Deborah You mean a man?

Danny Yes, a man.

Deborah I'm a Lesbian. (*Pause.*)

Danny As a physical preference, or from political beliefs?

Bernard's *apartment.* **Bernard** *is seated in front of the television at three in the morning.*

TV When you wish upon a star, makes no difference who you are. If, on the other hand, you apply for a personal loan, all sorts of circumstantial evidence is required. I wonder if any mathematician has done serious research on the efficacity of prayer. For example: you're walking down the street thinking 'God, if I don't get laid tonight, I don't know *what* all!' (A common form of prayer) And all of a sudden, WHAM! (*Pause.*) Perhaps you do get laid, or perhaps you get hit by a cab, or perhaps you meet the man or woman of your persuasion. But the prayer is uttered – yes it is – solely as a lamentation, and with no real belief in its causal properties.

When you don't get laid, tomorrow's prayer has the extra added oomph of involuntary continence. But if you do get laid – think on that a moment, will you? If you do manage to moisten the old wick, how many people would stop, before, during or after, and give thanks to a just creator?

Dan *and* **Deb** *are in bed at his apartment.*

Danny Well.

Deborah Well.

Danny Yeah, well, hey . . . uh . . . (*Pause.*) I feel *great.* (*Pause.*) You?

Deborah Uh huh.

Danny Yup. (*Pause.*) You, uh, you have to go to work (you work, right?) (**Deb** *nods.*) You have to go to work tomorrow?

Deborah Yes, well . . .

Danny You're going home?

Deborah Do you want me to?

Danny Only if you want to. Do you want to?

Deborah Do you want me to stay? I don't know if it's such a good idea that I stay here tonight.

Danny Why? (*Pause.*) I'd like you to stay. If you'd like to.

Deb *nods.*

Danny Well, then, all right, then. Huh? (*Pause.*)

Deborah I like your apartment.

Danny Yeah? I'm glad.

Deborah I like it here.

Danny So, look, so tell me. How would you like to eat dinner with me tomorrow. If you're not doing anything. If you're not too busy. If you're busy it's not important.

Deborah I'd love to eat dinner with you tomorrow.

Danny You would, huh?

Deborah Yes.

Danny Well, okay, that's nice. That's very nice. I'm going to look forward to that.

Deborah I could come over here and cook.

Danny You could.

Deborah Yes.

Danny You could come over here and cook dinner, you'd like to do that?

Deborah Yes.

Danny We could do that . . .

Deborah Sure.

Danny Yeah. We could do that. (*Pause.*) Let's do that.

Deborah Okay. (*Pause.*) I'm not really a Lesbian.

Danny No?

Deborah But I have had some Lesbianic experiences.

Danny What, like going to bed with other women?

Deborah . . . and I enjoyed them.

Danny (*pause*) Well, sure. (*Pause.*) You going to sleep?

Deborah (*sleepily*) Yes.

Danny (*pause*) You having a good time?

Deborah (*sleeping*) Yes.

Danny That's good. (*Pause.*) Goodnight.

Deborah Goodnight.

Pause.

Danny See you in the morning.

The next morning. **Deb** *and* **Joan** *at their apartment.* **Deb** *enters.*

Joan So what's he like?

Deborah Who?

Joan Whoever you haven't been home, I haven't seen you in two days that you've been seeing.

Deborah Did you miss me?

Joan No. Your plants died. (*Pause.*) I'm kidding. What's his name.

Deborah Danny.

Joan What's he do?

Deborah He works in the Loop.

Joan How wonderful for him.

Deborah He's an Assistant Office Manager.

Joan That's nice, a job with a little upward mobility.

Deborah Don't be like that, Joan.

Joan I'm sorry. I don't know what got into me.

Deborah How are things at school?

Joan Swell. Life in the Primary Grades is a real picnic. The other kindergarten teacher got raped Tuesday.

Deborah How terrible.

Joan What?

Deborah How terrible for her.

Joan Well, *of course* it was terrible for her. Good Christ, Deborah, you really amaze me sometimes, you know that?

A bar. **Bernard** *is seated at the bar; he is waiting.*

Bernie What do you have to do to get a drink in this place, come on a cracker?

Dan *and* **Deb** *appear at the entrance to the bar.*

Danny You're going to like Bernie, you're going to like him a lot. Ah! Ask him to tell you about Korea, he has got some stories you are not going to believe.

Bernard *spots them.*

Bernie Yo! Siddown, siddown, so what are you having?

They all sit down at a table.

Danny Deborah?

Deborah Jack Daniels on the Rocks.

Bernie So she knows what she's talking about, huh? (*To Deb*.) Black or Green?

Deborah Black.

Bernie *Okay*. And you?

Danny The same.

Bernie Right back. (*He goes to bar.*)

Danny Well, that's Bernie.

Deborah Seems like a nice enough sort of fellow.

Danny *Hell* of a guy.

Deborah Is he coming with us to the movies?

Bernard *reappears with drinks.*

Bernie So, actually, I'm Bernard Litko; friend and associate of your pal, Danny. And you're Deborah.

Deborah Deborah Soloman.

Bernie Danny's been telling me a lot about you.

Deborah We only met Wednesday.

Bernie He talks about you constantly.

Deborah No!

Bernie Yes.

Deborah What does he say?

Bernie All the usual things.

Pause.

Danny Bernie was in Korea.

Deborah Really?

Bernie Yeah. You see M*A*S*H on TV? (*Pause.*) It all looks like that. There isn't one square inch of Korea that doesn't look like that. (*Pause.*) I'm not kidding. (*Pause.*)

Deborah When were you there?

Bernie '67.

Deborah Really? What were you doing in Korea in 1967?

Pause.

Bernie I'm not really at liberty to talk about it.

Pause.

So what do you do?

Deborah I'm an illustrator.

Bernie Commercial artist, huh?

Deborah Yes.

Bernie Lots of money in that. I mean, that's a hell of a field for a girl.

Danny She's very good at it.

Bernie I don't doubt it for a second. I mean, *look* at her for chrissakes. You're a very attractive woman. Anybody ever tell you that? (*Pause.*) So (*Pause.*) So okay, so what sign are you?

Deborah Scorpio.

Bernie Scorpio, huh? . . . Scorpio . . . how about that.

Deborah What sign are *you*?

Bernie Scorpio.

Deborah How about that. Danny's a Scorpio.

Bernie You a Scorpio, Dan?

Danny Yes. (*Pause.*)

Bernie Well, I don't want to say it, but it's a small fucking world. (*Pause.*) So you guys are hitting it off, huh? The two of you, you're hitting it on/off?

Deborah Well . . .

Bernie What the hell, it's early. (*To* **Dan**.) You don't even know if she's a keeper yet, for chrissakes. You're young. What the hell. (*To* **Deb**.) How old are you?

Danny Bernie, you know you're not supposed to ask a woman her age.

Bernie Dan. Dan, these are modern times. What do you think this is, *the past*? Women are liberated. You got a right to be what age you are, and so do I, and so does Deborah. (*To* **Deb**.) Right?

Deborah Oh, I suppose so.

Bernie So what are you? Eighteen . . . nineteen.

Deborah Actually, I'm twenty-three.

Bernie Well, you don't look it. (*Pause.*) You know, you're a lucky guy, Dan. And I think you know what I'm taking about. You are one lucky guy. Yes sir, you are one fortunate son of a bitch. And I think I know what I'm talking about.

Dan *and* **Bernard** *are filing at the office.*

Bernie One thing, and I want to tell you that if everybody thought of this, Dan, we could do away with income tax (hand me one of those 12-12's, will ya?), there

would be no more war (thanks), and you and I could
dwell in Earthly Paradise today. (*Pause.*)

Danny What?

Bernie Just this:

Danny Yeah?

Bernie That when she's on her back, her legs are in the
air, she's coming like a choo-choo and she's screaming
'don't stop' . . .

Danny Yeah?

Bernie I want you to remember . . .

Danny . . . yeah? . . .

Bernie That power . . . (*Pause.*) . . . that *power* means
responsibility. (*Pause.*) Remember that.

Danny I will.

Pause.

Bernie Good.

Outside **Deb** *and* **Joan**'s *apartment.* **Joan** *is leaving the
apartment.* **Dan** *runs into her in the hall.*

Danny Hi.

Joan Hello.

Danny I'm looking for Deborah.

Joan She's not here now.

Danny Oh. What is she, out?

Joan She's out.

Danny I'm supposed to meet her here.

Joan Well, she's not here now. (*Pause.*)

Danny Well, perhaps we could stand out here and tell

each other funny stories until she got back. What do you think?

Joan Was she expecting you?

Danny I'm supposed to meet her here.

Joan You were supposed to meet her here when?

Danny Now.

Joan What time did she say?

Danny Around seven.

Joan Well, I'll tell her you stopped by.

Danny Wait. Wait . . . what? Could I have a chair or something? I'll be glad to wait outside the door. Maybe if you just have a stool and a copy of *Boy's Life* or something I could read. (*Pause.*) Why are you being so hostile?

Joan I don't like your attitude. (*Pause.*)

Danny My name is Danny Shapiro.

Joan I know who you are.

Dan *and* **Bernard**'*s office. They are filing.*

Danny You ever do it in a plane?

Bernie Yup.

Danny Underwater?

Bernie Yup.

Danny You ever do it in a movie?

Bernie Yes I have, Dan. I believe I have, yes. (*Pause.*) You know what some of 'em like? They like you to get a trifle off the beaten track, if you know what I mean. I had this one chick, she used to have me wrap her in a bicycle chain and lock her to the radiator before she'd let me do it.

Danny Yeah?

Bernie Spent five months with that broad before it got cold. A lot of them. They like you to get off the beaten track.

Danny Yeah?

Bernie *Oh* yeah. Read your history. The Ancient Greeks . . . the French . . . you heard of King Farouk?

Danny Yeah.

Bernie King Farouk, now one of the shots, I read, he'd pull into some small town, Dubuque, Peoria . . . he'd go put the make on some waitress.

Danny Yeah.

Bernie So after work, they'd all go back to her place and start making it.

Danny Uh huh.

Bernie The shot of it was this: now secretly, while she was still at work, his men would go divert the local railroad . . .

Danny Yeah . . .

Bernie . . . and lay the tracks so they went right through the chick's house. Right by the headboard of her bed and out again on the main line.

Danny Uh huh.

Bernie So just as she's ready to come . . .

Danny Yeah.

Bernie The King gives a signal, his men run a locomotive right through the broad's bedroom.

Danny No.

Bernie Yeah. The broads loved it. The thing of it was this:

Danny Yeah.

Bernie King Farouk was a bit kinky. Right?

Danny Right?

Bernie So get this: There they're humping and bumping
. . . the chick's about to come . . .

Danny Yeah.

Bernie She hears 'Chugga chugga chugga,' and then
wham, the house caves in.

Danny Uh huh.

Bernie So she sits up in bed, she says 'What's that?', the
King goes 'That my dear, is a choo-choo' . . .

Danny Uh huh.

Bernie Then he whacks her on the forehead with a ball-
peen hammer.

Danny No shit.

Bernie Yeah.

Pause.

Danny How'd he get away with it?

Bernie You shitting me? The King had emissaries all
over the country, they'd fix it up so it looked like the chick
had got hit by a train.

Pause.

He'd take care of their families, though.

Danny The girls' families.

Bernie Yeah. He'd send them a couple g's. A g or two in
savings bonds.

Pause.

Danny He could afford it.

Bernie Are you shitting me? The man was king of *Egypt*. (*Pause.*) A *huge* fucking country.

Danny Yeah.

Bernie An ancient land.

Danny Yeah.

Pause.

Bernie So tell me.

Danny What?

Bernie How are you getting along with that girl?

Danny What girl?

Bernie You introduced me to.

Danny Deborah?

Bernie Deborah, Betty, whatever.

Danny Her name's Deborah.

Bernie I don't know that? I know what her name is, I'm asking you how you're getting on.

Danny We're getting on just fine. (*Pause.*)

Bernie That's okay. (*Pause.*) You don't want to talk about it, we won't think about it.

Danny I didn't say I didn't want to talk about it.

Pause.

Bernie Does she give head?

Danny What?

Bernie To you, I'm saying. Does she give head to *you*.

Pause.

Forget it.

Danny You want me to do these 12-12's?

Bernie Yeah, do'em. Do'em. (*Pause.*)

Danny You ever make it with an Oriental?

Bernie No. I spent eighteen months in Korea jacking off. Do the 12-12's, huh?

Joan *and* **Deb**'s *apartment. The evening. They are sitting around.*

Joan I don't know, I don't know. I don't know, I don't know. I don't know. (*Pause.*)

Deborah You don't know what?

Joan I don't know anything, Deborah, I swear to god, the older I get the less I know. (*Pause.*) It's a puzzle. Our efforts at coming to grips with ourselves . . . in an attempt to become 'more human' (which, in itself is an interesting concept). It has to do with an increased ability to recognize *clues* . . . and the control of energy in the form of *lust* . . . and *desire* . . . (And also in the form of hope.)

But a *finite* puzzle. Whose true solution lies, perhaps, in transcending the rules themselves . . . (*Pause.*) . . . and pounding of the fucking pieces into places where they DO NOT FIT AT ALL.

Pause.

Those of us who have seen the hands of the Master Magician move a bit too slowly do have a rough time from time to time.

Pause.

Some things persist. (*Pause.*) 'Loss' is always possible . . .

Pause.

Phone rings.

Deborah I'll take it in the other room. (*Goes.*)

Dan *and* **Bernard***'s office. Closing up.* **Dan** *and* **Bernard** *are securing the office at the end of the day.*

Bernie So what are we doing tomorrow, we going to the beach?

Danny I'm seeing Deborah.

Bernie Yeah? You getting serious? I mean seemed like a hell of a girl, huh? The little I saw of her. Not too this, not too that . . . very kind of . . . what? (*Pause.*) Well, what the fuck. I only saw her for a minute. I mean first impressions of this kind are often misleading, huh? So what can you tell from seeing a broad one, two, ten times. You're seeing a lot of this broad. You getting serious? But what the fuck, that's your business. Right?

Danny Umm.

Bernie So what are you guys going to do, maybe . . . what? Go to the zoo, or shopping? . . . She looked very intellectual.

Danny Um.

Bernie That's not always a bad thing.

Danny No.

Bernie I mean what the fuck, a guy wants to get it on with some broad on a more or less stable basis, who is to say him no. (*Pause.*) A lot of these broads, you know, you just don't know. You know? I mean what with where they've been and all. I mean a young woman in today's society . . . time she's twenty two-three. You don't know *where* the fuck she's been. (*Pause.*) I'm just *talking* to you, you understand.

Dan*'s apartment.* **Dan** *and* **Deb** *are in bed.*

Danny So tell me.

Deborah What?

Danny Everything. Tell me the *truth* about everything. Menstruation. I know you're holding out on me.

Deborah It would be hard on me if it got out.

Danny I swear.

Deborah It's under our conscious control.

Danny I knew it!

Deborah We just do it to drive you crazy with the mess.

Danny I just knew it . . .

Deborah Now you tell me some.

Danny Name it.

Deborah What does it feel like to have a penis?

Danny Strange. Very strange and wonderful.

Deborah Do you miss having tits?

Danny To be completely frank with you, that is the stupidest question I ever heard. What man in his right mind would want tits?

Deborah You're right of course. (*Pause.*) Ask me if I like the taste of come.

Danny Do you like the taste of come?

Deborah Do I like the taste of come?

Danny Yes.

Deborah Dan, I love the taste of come. It tastes like everything . . . *good* . . . just . . . *coming* out of your cock . . . the Junior Prom . . . an autumn afternoon . . .

Danny It doesn't taste a little bit like Chlorox?

Deborah It *smells* like Chlorox. It tastes like the Junior Prom. (*Pause.*) See what you cheat yourself of?

Danny Yes.

Deborah Faggot. (*Pause.*)

Danny Do you ever fantasize about making love with other women?

Deborah Do you fantasize when we make love? (*Pause.*) The last time we made love, I fantasized about other women.

Danny The last time I masturbated I kept thinking about my left hand.

Deborah Did you?

Danny Yes.

Deborah Did you?

Danny Yes.

Pause.

I love making love with you.

Deborah I love making love with you. (*Pause.*)

Danny I love you.

Deborah Does it frighten you to say that?

Danny Yes.

Deborah It's only words. I don't think you should be frightened by words.

Nursery School. **Joan** *is lecturing two toddlers.*

Joan What are you doing? Where are you going? What are you doing? You stay right there. Now. What were the two of you doing? I'm just asking a simple question. There's nothing to be ashamed of. (*Pause.*) I can wait. Were you playing 'Doctor'? (*Pause.*) 'Doctor.' Don't play dumb with me, just answer the question. (You know, that attitude is going to get you in a lot of trouble someday.) Were you playing with each other's genitals? Each other's . . . 'pee-pees'? . . . whatever you call them at home, that's what I'm asking (and don't play dumb, because I saw what you were doing, so just own up to it). (*Pause.*) All right . . . no. No, stop that, there's no reason for tears . . . it's perfectly . . . natural. But . . . there's a time and a place for everything. Now . . . no, it's all right. Come on. Come on, we're all going in the other room, and we're going to wash our hands. And then Miss Webber is going to call our parents.

The Toy Department at Marshall Field's. **Bernard** *and* **Dan** *are shopping for a gift.*

Danny Whose birthday?

Bernie My nephew Bobby.

Danny How old is he now?

Bernie Going to be . . . six. Will you look at that?

Danny What?

Bernie They got a fucking fruit at the games counter. I can't believe this. In the midst of the toy department. At the games counter, talking to the kids all day long . . . a fairy.

Danny Yeah.

Bernie You know, one of those motherfuckers grabbed me when I was Bobby's age.

Danny Where?

Bernie At the movies, where else? We're all wondering what this old guy is doing at the cartoons, and he sits down at the end of the row, and halfway through he reaches over and grabs my joint. Reaches over *another* guy and grabs *me* by the joint.

Danny Was he rough?

Bernie What?

Danny I mean, was he rough about it?

Bernie Rough? (*Pause.*) I mean . . . (*Pause.*) Rough? What difference *how* he grabbed me? I mean, he's a *guy*.

Danny Yeah.

Bernie And *I'm* a guy. (*Pause.*) But at the time I was only a *kid*, for chrissakes. (*Pause.*)

Danny You ever do that stuff when you were kids?

Bernie What stuff?

Danny You know. Stuff with other kids.

Bernie Teasing? Like teasing the girls? Looking up their panties and so on?

Danny No, I mean when you were really young kids. Fooling around with the other kids . . . the other boys.

Bernie Fooling around? You mean like 'messing' around with other boys?

Danny Fuck no. I didn't mean that. I just meant . . . you know.

Bernie (*Pause.*) You mean fooling *around*! Sure, who didn't.

Danny Yeah.

Bernie Shit, we all used to fuck around.

Danny Right.

Bernie Even when we were little, shit. I mean you *learn* when you're young, right?

Danny Right.

Bernie And what you *learn*, that's what you *know*. Am I right?

Danny One Hundred Percent. It's all in your . . .

Bernie Head.

Danny . . . approach (*Pause.*)

Bernie It's in your what?

Danny Approach?

Bernie Right.

Danny You know how to approach these things and you'll always be all right.

Bernie You don't learn right when you're young, those cocksuckers ruin your life.

Danny Who? (*Pause.*)

Bernie Anybody. (*Pause.*) Ruin it quicker'n you can turn around.

Danny Take you and that guy in the movies, for instance.

Bernie What do you mean?

Danny Just that if you'd been a little *older* . . .

Bernie Yeah?

Danny Or maybe the guy, if he'd been a little . . . younger . . .

Bernie What are you fucking talking about?

Danny I'm saying that if the circumstances . . .

Bernie What fucking circumstances? Some faggot queer got the hots for my joint at the cartoons.

Danny I'm not talking about *extenuating* circumstances, I only mean the circumstances of what happened.

Bernie And what exactly are you saying about them?

Danny All I'm saying . . .

Bernie . . . this happened *years* ago . . .

Danny . . . is that it could possibly have been damaging to you. (*Pause.*)

Bernie Yeah?

Danny . . . as a total Human Being.

Bernie Damn right.

Danny . . . and you're just lucky that it didn't.

Bernie Well, what the fuck, I was only a kid.

Danny Sure.

Bernie A kid laughs these things off. You forget, you go on living . . . what the fuck, huh?

Deb and **Joan**'s *apartment. Late at night. They are lounging.*

Joan Let's face it. He would prematurely ejaculate. There's no nicer way to say it. And the sooner he would come the guiltier he would feel and the sooner he would come. Because in some ways, of course, he was doing it to punish me. And he was doing a hell of a job of it.

So one day I said to him 'Look, I'm in bed to make love with you, and you're in bed to make love with me. So why don't we just relax, and I'll be with you, and you be with me, and whenever you want to come is fine.' (*Pause.*) But he still kept prematurely ejaculating. (*Pause.*) Although he did seem happier about it. (*Pause.*)

Tableau.

Deborah We have any tuna fish?

Joan I think I ate it. (*Tableau.*)

The Health Club. **Bernard** *in the gym talking to imaginary buddies.*

Bernie So the kid asks me 'Bernie blah, blah, blah, blah, blah, blah, blah, blah, blah, blah. The broad *this*, the broad *that*, blah blah blah.' Right? So I tell him, 'Dan, Dan, you think I don't know what you're feeling, I don't know what you're going through? You think about the

broad, you *this*, you *that*, you think I don't know that?' So
he tells me, 'Bernie,' he says, 'I think I love her.' (*Pause.*)
Twenty-eight years old.

So I tell him, 'Dan, Dan, I can *advise*, I can *counsel*, I can
speak to you out of my *experience* . . . but in the final
analysis, you are on your own. (*Pause.*) If you want my
opinion, however, you are pussy-whipped.' (I call 'em like I
see 'em. I wouldn't say it if it wasn't so.) So what does he
know at that age, huh? Sell his soul for a little eating
pussy, and who can blame him. But mark my words: one,
two more weeks, he'll do the right thing by the broad.
(*Pause.*) And drop her like a fucking hot potato.

Joan *and* **Deb** *are out to lunch.*

Joan . . . and, of course, there exists the very real
possibility that the whole thing is nothing other than a
mistake of *rather* large magnitude, and that it never *was*
supposed to work out.

Deborah Do you really believe that?

Joan I don't know. I really don't know. I think I *do*. Well,
look at your divorce rate. Look at the incidence of
homosexuality . . . the number of violent, sex-connected
crimes (this dressing is for shit) . . . all the antisocial
behaviour that chooses sex as its form of expression. Eh?

Deborah I don't know.

Joan . . . physical and mental mutilations we perpetrate
on each other, day in, day out . . . trying to fit ourselves
to a pattern we can neither *understand* (although we
pretend to) nor truly afford to *investigate* (although we
pretend to). (*Pause.*) Come on, disagree with me.

Deborah I disagree with you.

Joan It's a dirty joke, Deborah, the whole godforsaken
business.

Deborah I disagree with you.

Joan That's your right. Are you going to eat your roll? (**Deb** *shakes her head.*) Then perhaps *I* could have it. (*Takes roll.*) This roll is excellent.

Deborah I'm moving in with Danny.

Joan I give you two months.

Dan *and* **Bernard**'s *office.* **Dan** *is filing.* **Bernard** *is talking on the phone.*

Bernie . . . so then she brings the dog in. 'What's the pooch for?' I say. 'Shut up and watch,' she says. 'You might learn something.' . . . at the Laugh-Inn. (*Pause.*) They're open all night. (*Pause.*) No, they don't. (*Pause.*) I'm telling you they're open all night.

Danny They're open all night, Bern.

Bernie (*to phone*) I'm sorry. (*To* **Dan**.) What?

Danny They're open all night.

Bernie Yeah. (*To phone.*) They're open all night. (*Pause.*) A guy in the office. So then she gets down on the carpet with the dog . . .

Danny You want me to do these 11'13's?

Bernie (*to* **Dan**) Yeah. (*To phone.*) So I'm just watching at this point. (*Pause.*) I'm getting to that. So the fucking dog, and may I be struck dead by lightning, his eyes light up, and he starts to grin . . . (*Pause.*) . . . a fox terrier.

Dan *and* **Deb** *move* **Deb** *out of her apartment.* **Joan** *is in the background.*

Danny You have very interesting taste in music.

Deborah A lot of them are Joan's.

Danny I'm sorry . . . uh . . . (*To* **Joan**.) uh, which of these are yours? You want to separate them?

Joan Well, they aren't going to separate themselves, now, are they?

Danny No, I don't suppose they are. Why don't *you* separate them, Joan? (*Pause.*)

Deborah Danny has a sauna in his building.

Joan How nice . . . sweating . . . Do you use your sauna often, Danny?

Danny I use the sauna from time to time. I'm fortunate in being blessed with the ability to sweat in the everyday course of events.

Deborah (*to* **Joan**) What are we going to do about the television?

Joan Do you want to take it?

Danny I have a television.

Joan Let me just pay you for your half of it.

Deborah You could send me a cheque.

Joan I could *give* you a cheque. You're not going to California for God's sake.

Deborah I can pick it up next week.

Joan When?

Deborah Whenever is convenient.

Joan Can you come by Tuesday night? . . . (*To* **Dan**.) Can she come by Tuesday night?

Danny That's very good. That's very funny. Now could you find it in your heart to take the table lamp and shove it up your ass?

Joan Ah, that's very telling. On your instructions, I'm supposed to rend and torture myself anally. Is that what you like? Does Deborah know about this? You're moving out, move out.

Danny She's moving out.

Joan Well, move *her* out, then and the hell with you. (*Pause. To* **Deb**.) I hope you're very happy.

Bernard *is at the office declaiming to some co-workers.*

Bernie Equal Rights Amendment? Equal Rights Amendment? I'll give you the fucking Equal Rights Amendment. Nobody ever wrote *me* no fucking amendments. Special *interest* groups, *okay* . . . but who's kidding who here, huh? (*Pause.*) We got baby seals dying in Alaska and we're writing amendments for *broads*? I mean, I'm a big fan of *society* . . . but this bites the big one. I'm sorry.

Dan *and* **Deb**'s *apartment. The morning. They are each getting ready for work.*

Danny Do we have any shampoo?

Deborah I don't know.

Danny You wash your hair at least twice a day. Shampoo is a staple item of your existence. Of course you know.

Deborah All right. I *do*. Know.

Danny Do we have any shampoo?

Deborah I don't know. Is your hair dirty?

Danny Does my hair look dirty?

Deborah Does it feel dirty? (*Pause.*) It looks dirty.

Danny It feels greasy. I hate it when my hair feels greasy.

Deborah Well, I'm not going to look. If you want to know if there's any shampoo, you go look for it.

Danny You don't have to look. You know very well if there's any shampoo or not. You're making me be ridiculous about this. (*Pause.*) You wash yourself too much anyway. If you really *used* all that shit they tell you in *Cosmopolitan* (and you do) you'd be washing yourself from morning till night. Pouring derivatives on yourself all day long.

Deborah Will you love me when I'm old?

Danny If you can manage to look eighteen, yes.

Deborah Now, that's very telling.

Danny You think so?

Deborah Yes.

Danny I'm going to wash my hair. Is there any shampoo?

Deborah Yes. And no.

Danny Now what's that supposed to mean?

Deborah Everything. And nothing. (*Pause.*) Would you get my hose?

Danny No. Where does this come from? This whole fucking behaviour. You're making it up. 'Get my hose.' You want your hose, I'll get your hose. Here's your fucking hose. (*Rummages in dresser.*) Where's your hose? (*Pause.*) What do they call them, anyway? Nobody says 'hose.'

Deborah Pantyhose.

Danny Where are they?

Deborah Get me some out of the laundry bag.

Danny You're going to wear dirty hose?

Deborah I think I'm out of clean ones.

Danny So you're going downtown in dirty hose?

Deborah Do you want me walking around with a naked la-la?

Danny If it makes you happy, Deb. I'm on the side of whatever makes you happy.

Deb *retrieves dirty hose from bag and starts changing into them.*

Danny You make me very horny.

Deborah It's the idea of the dirty panties, Dan. You're sick.

Danny I love your breasts.

Deborah 'Thank you.' (*Pause.*) Is that right?

Danny Fuck you.

Deborah No hard feelings.

Danny Who said there were?

Deborah You know there are.

Danny Then why say there aren't?

Dan's *office.* **Dan** *is talking to an imaginary co-worker.*

Danny . . . no, wait a second. Wait a second. I want to tell you this. I know what you're saying, and I'm telling you I don't like you bad mouthing the guy, who happens to be a friend of mine. So just let me tell my story, okay?

So the other day we're up on six and it's past five and I'm late, and I'm having some troubles with my chick (this chick I've been seeing) and I push the button and the elevator doesn't come, and it doesn't come, and it doesn't come, so I lean back and I kick the shit out of it three or four times (I was really hot). And *he*, he puts his arm around my shoulder and he calms me down and he says, 'Dan, Dan . . . don't go looking for affection from inanimate objects.' (*Pause.*) Huh? (*Pause.*) So I don't want to hear you badmouthing Bernie Litko.

Dan *and* **Deb** *in bed late at night.* **Deb** *is sleeping.*

Danny Deborah. Deb? Deb? You up?

Pause.

You sleeping?

Pause.

I can't sleep.

Pause.

You asleep?

Pause.

Huh?

Pause.

You sleeping, Deb?

Pause.

What are you thinking about?

Pause.

Deb?

Pause.

Did I wake you up?

A movie theatre. **Dan** *and* **Bernard** *are watching a pornographic movie.*

Bernie Don't tell me that's that guy's joint. Whatever you do don't tell me that. That's not his joint. Tell me it's not his joint, Dan.

Danny It's his joint.

Bernie I don't want to hear it.

Danny That's what it is.

Bernie I don't want to hear it, so don't tell it to me. Nobody is hung like that. If that's his joint I'm going to go home and blow my brains out.

Danny He probably used a stand-in. (*Pause.*)

Bernie I can't stand this. I can't fucking stand this. *Lookit* that broad!

Danny Which one?

Bernie Which *one*? The one she looks a bit like whatsername.

Danny Like Deborah?

Bernie Yeah.

Danny Which one is that?

Bernie That one.

Danny You think she looks like Deborah?

Bernie Yeah. You see what I mean?

Danny No. You think she's *pretty*?

Bernie Pretty? What the fuck are you talking about? (*Pause.*) You know this fucking house has changed.

Danny Yeah.

Bernie I mean, they still got the guys jerkin' off under the *Trib* in the front row . . .

Danny World's Greatest Newspaper.

Bernie . . . but they got a lot of scum in here now. Wait, now. Wait. Do you see that. Will you look at the fucking that?

Danny What?

Bernie That break in the action . . . they shifted scenes . . . where they changed the camera angle . . . you know why they do that? You know why? Because the guy *came* is why, and they shift angles and wait a while so it looks like he's fucking for hours. You see that?

Danny Yeah.

Bernie These guys got no control. (*Pause.*) What was I saying?

Danny How the house has changed.

Bernie They got a lot of scum in here now. DO YOU SEE *THAT*? DO YOU FUCKING BELIEVE THAT? (*Pause.*) A woman blowing a man's natural. A woman blowing a dog's disgusting. (*Pause.*) Yeah, that's what I think, and I'm not ashamed to say it!

Dan *and* **Deb** *at their apartment. In the midst of an all-night argument.*

Deborah Oh, shut up.

Danny I should shut up? Who's talking for the last twelve hours straight, huh?

Deborah *motions him away in disgust.*

. . . blah blah blah, blah blah blah, blah blah blah. Jesus. Some people go home with the *Tribune*. You go home with me. Everything's fine. Sex, talk, life, everything. Until you want to get 'closer,' to get 'better.' Do you know what the fuck you want?

Push. You push me.

Why can't you just see it for what it is?

Deborah What?

Danny Us.

Deborah And what is it?

Danny What it *is*, no more no less.

Deborah And what is that?

Danny Don't give me this. Don't give me that look. Missy.

Deborah Or you're gonna what?

Danny I don't mind physical violence. I just can't stand emotional violence. (*Pause.*) I'm sorry. I'm sorry Deb. (*Pause.*) I forget who I'm talking to. I'm sorry. You're very good for me, come here. (*Pause.*) Come here.

Deborah No. You come here for Christ's fucking sake. You want comfort, come get comfort. What am I, your toaster?

Danny Cunt.

Deborah That's very good. 'Cunt', good. Get it out. Let it all out.

Danny You cunt.

Deborah We've established that.

Danny I try.

Deborah You try and try. You are misunderstood and depressed.

Danny And you're no help.

Deborah No, I'm a hindrance. You're trying to understand women and I'm confusing you with information. 'Cunt' won't do it. 'Fuck' won't do it. No more magic. What are you *feeling*. Tell me what you're *feeling*. Jerk.

Deb *alone.*

Deborah My mother used to tell a story about how I came into the kitchen one day while she was preparing an important dish. I was about four. I said, 'Mommy, can I have a cookie?', and she for some reason misunderstood or misheard me, and thought that I said that I wanted a 'hug,' so she gave me a 'hug,' and I said 'Thank you, Mommy. I didn't want a cookie after all.'

(*Pause.*) You see? What is a sublimation of what? (*Pause.*) What signifies what?

Dan *at* **Bernard***'s apartment. The middle of the night. They are drunk.*

Bernie Tits and Ass. Tits and Ass. Tits and Ass. Tits and Ass. Blah de Bloo. Blah de Bloo. Blah de Bloo. Blah de Bloo. (*Pause.*) Huh?

Danny I don't know.

Bernie So *don't* know. Big deal – you are going to lose your head over a little bit of puss? You are going to sell your birthright for a mess of potash? 'Oh, Bernie, she's *this*. Oh, Bernie, she's *that* . . .' You know what she is? She's a fucking human being just like you and me, Dan. We all have basically the same desires, and the shame of it is you get out of touch with yourself and lose your perspective. Huh?

Pause.

Huh?

Yeah. You think you're playing with *kids*? (*Pause.*) Don't ever lose your sense of humour, Dan. Don't *ever* lose your sense of humour.

Dan *and* **Deb** *at their apartment. Splitting up their belongings.*

Danny . . . and your friend, Joan . . . that cunt was born in a carcrash. (*Pause.*) And your job is a lot of busy-work, you know that?

Deborah I know.

Danny And I have *no* fucking idea what your drawings mean. (*Pause.*) And you're a lousy fuck.

Deborah I know.

Danny Your friend, *Joan*, is a better fuck than *you* are.

Deborah I'm sure she is.

Danny . . . and *she's* a lousy fuck. (*Pause.*) Aren't you going to tell me I'm a lousy fuck?

Deborah You *are* a lousy fuck.

Danny You're fulla shit.

Deb *and* **Joan** *at their apartment.*

Joan You learn from your mistakes, Deborah. Man is the one animal who has that capacity.

Deborah Yes.

Joan You can't live in the past.

Deborah No.

Joan It does you no good.

Deborah I know it.

Joan And, in the end, what do you have? You have your friends. (*Pause.*) Have you been drawing since you've been with Dan?

Deborah It wasn't his fault.

Joan Well, whose fault was it, *mine*?

Deborah It was my fault, Joan.

Joan It was not your fault. Say what you will, the *facts* don't change and the fact is if you take a grown man whose actions and whose outlook are those of a child, who wants nothing more or better than to have someone who

will lick his penis and grin at his bizarre idea of wit, uh
. . . if you take that man and uh . . .

Deborah I'll thank you for this someday.

Joan Yes, you will, Deb. And you know, I truly don't see
why you're being so hostile. I'm afraid I have to admit
that.

Joan *is reading a story to her imaginary toddlers.*

Joan . . . and when the Prince came home that night, she
had changed into an old Hag (so of course he was very
surprised).
'Where is my beautiful wife?' he asked the Hag.
'And what have you done with her?' And she said, 'I am
your wife.'
(That's right.)
'I can be beautiful during the daylight hours so that you
and your friends can admire me, or I can be beautiful at
night, so that you can enjoy me by the fireside, and so on.
But for one half of the day I must be this old Hag you see
before you.'

Pause.

A 'hag' is an ugly old lady.

Pause.

Well, how do you think it's spelled?

Pause.

Well, how does it sound?

Pause.

That's right. And so she told him . . .

Dan *and* **Bernard** *are on the beach. They are looking at attractive women.*

Bernie Lookit this.

Danny Where?

Bernie *Lookit* this.

Danny Where?

Bernie There.

Danny *Oh* yeah.

Bernie My sweet goodness.

Danny Uh huh.

Bernie What a sensitive young lady.

Danny Check this one out.

Bernie Don't bother me.

Danny I'm telling you.

Bernie Where?

Danny Two o'clock.

Bernie (*looks*) Oh *no*!

Danny Yes.

Bernie Oh *no*!

Danny I'm afraid so.

Bernie I see no reason to go on living.

Danny Ummm.

Bernie There can be no more to life.

Danny Yes.

Bernie In a way it's sad. To think I gaze upon the highest man can wish for . . .

Danny Bernie . . .

Bernie His destiny . . .

Danny Bernie . . .

Bernie The fruition of a pain-laden stay on earth . . .

Danny Hey, Bernie, isn't that whatsername?

Bernie Her?

Danny Yeah.

Bernie Is she who?

Danny *What*zername, who you introduced me to last week.

Bernie Naaa. This broad is much better looking.

Danny I think it's her.

Bernie This broad has a lot more class.

Danny No . . .

Bernie Lookit her boobs. (*Pause.*) Am I right or not?

Danny Yeah, I think you're right.

Bernie Hey! Don't look behind you.

Danny Yeah?

Bernie Whatever you do, don't look behind you.

Danny Where?

Bernie Right behind you, about ten feet behind you to your right.

Danny Yeah?

Bernie I'm telling you.

Danny (*looks*) Get the fuck *outta* here!

Bernie Can I pick 'em?

Danny Bernie . . .

Bernie Is the radar in fine shape?

Danny . . . I gotta say . . .

Bernie . . . *Oh* yeah . . .

Danny . . . that you can *pick* 'em.

Bernie I know I can. And will you look at the chick in the two piece wet-look jobbie?

Danny Where?

Bernie Where I'm looking. (*Pause.*) Those *legs* . . .

Danny Oh *no*!

Bernie . . . all the way up to her *ass*!

Danny Jesus.

Bernie And *beyond* for all we know.

Danny You said it.

Bernie *Look*it her.

Danny Yup.

Bernie Fuckin' *look*it her.

Danny I know it.

Bernie Tell me she is not flaunting herself all over the beach.

Danny She is casting it to the winds.

Bernie Look at that *suit*.

Danny Bern . . . Bernie . . . I think that I can see her snatch.

Bernie You're fulla shit.

Danny On my honour. I can see her fucking snatch.

Bernie You can see her snatch?

Danny I'm telling you.

Bernie (*looks*) I can't make it out.

Danny At the top of her legs.

Bernie I known where it is, I just can't see it.

Danny When she breathes in. You gotta look close.

Pause. They look.

Bernie Where does she get off with that noise?

Danny Yeah.

Bernie That fuckin' pisses me off.

Danny Yeah.

Bernie That pisses the *fuck* off outta me.

Danny I know.

Bernie Piss.

Danny Cockteaser.

Bernie Prissy little cunt.

Danny Right on the beach.

Bernie Piss me off.

Danny Little prude.

Bernie On the fucking beach.

Danny And those *tits*!

Bernie Don't talk to me about tits.

Danny Nice firm tits.

Bernie Where does she get off with those tits?

Danny What a pair of boobs.

Bernie Not that I'm a tit man . . .

Danny I know.

Bernie I mean, I *dig* tits . . .

Danny I don't blame you.

Bernie . . . but I wouldn't go out of my way for a pair of tits.

Danny Yeah.

Bernie The way I see it, *tits* . . .

Danny Yeah?

Bernie . . . are what you make of 'em.

Danny It's like anything else.

Bernie But an *ass* . . .

Danny Yeah.

Bernie . . . is an *ass*.

Danny Goes without saying. You know what I like?

Bernie What?

Danny Stomach muscles.

Bernie You're talking about flab.

Danny Yeah.

Bernie I know what you're talking about.

Danny I know you do.

Bernie Flab.

Danny Fuckin' flab.

Bernie Who needs it?

Danny More trouble than it's worth.

Bernie A nice pair of legs though . . .

Danny I know it.

Bernie . . . is like money from home.

Danny A home *away* from home.

Bernie Now look over there to illustrate my point.

Danny The broad?

Bernie Right. Nice legs, eh?

Danny Yup.

Bernie Very acceptable old ass . . .

Danny Nice, firm.

Bernie Flat belly, beautiful pair of tits.

Danny No question.

Bernie Now *she* is fine. (*Pause.*)

Danny Right.

Bernie But now look over *there*. The broad with the dumpy legs and the fat whatdayacallit.

Danny Stomach.

Bernie Her legs are for shit, her stomach is dumpy, her tits don't say anything for her, and her muscle tone is not good.

Danny Right.

Bernie Now she is *not* a good-looking girl. (*Pause.*) In fact she is something of a pig. (*Pause.*) You see? That's all it takes . . . to make the difference between a knockout looking broad, and a nothing looking broad who doesn't look like anything. (*Pause.*) You see my point?

Danny . . . yeah?

Bernie Makes all the fucking difference in the world. (*Pause.*) Coming out here on the beach. Lying all over the beach, flaunting their bodies . . . I mean who the fuck do they think they are all of a sudden, coming out here and just flaunting their bodies all over? (*Pause.*) I mean, what are you supposed to think? I come to the beach with a friend to get some sun and watch the action and . . . I mean a fellow comes to the beach to sit out in the fucking sun, am I wrong? . . . I mean we're talking about

recreational fucking space, huh? . . . huh? (*Pause.*) What
the fuck am I talking about?

Danny Are you feeling all right?

Bernie Well, how do I look, do I look all right?

Danny Sure.

Bernie Well, then let's assume that I feel all right, okay?

Danny Okay.

Bernie I mean, how could you feel anything *but* all right,
for chrissakes? Will you look at that body? (*Pause.*) What a
pair of tits. (*Pause.*) With tits like that, who needs . . .
anything.

*A long pause. They watch an imaginary woman pass in front of
them.*

Bernie Hi.

Danny Hello there.

Pause. She walks by.

Bernie She's probably deaf.

Danny She did *look* deaf, didn't she.

Bernie Yeah. (*Pause.*)

Danny Deaf *bitch*.

Squirrels

This play is dedicated to
Linda Kimbrough

'Like a snake
I'm on the make'

Squirrels was first produced by the St. Nicholas Theatre Company, Chicago, October 1974, with the following cast:

Arthur	W. H. Macy
Edmond	Stephen Schachter
The Cleaning Woman	Linda Kimbrough

Directed by David Mamet

Note:
Some portions of the dialogue appear in parentheses, which serve to mark a slight change of outlook on the part of the speaker – perhaps a momentary change to a more introspective regard – D.M.

The Characters:
Arthur, *an old writer*
Edmond, *a young writer*
A Cleaning Woman

The Scene:
A writer's office

> 'The reason I like
> Edna St. Vincent Millay
> Is that her name.
> Sounds like a basketball
> Falling downstairs.
> The reason I like
> Walt Whitman
> Is that his name
> Sounds like
> Edna St. Vincent Millay
> Falling downstairs.'

Prologue

At rise: *The* **Cleaning Woman** *enters the office. She finds a crumpled up piece of paper on the floor, picks it up and reads it.*

Cleaning Woman Squirrels. (*Shows it to audience.*) What is this thing he's got for squirrels, for Chrissake? Ah, I don't know. (*Tosses it in wastebasket.*) Let me tell you something. Live in the past, live in the future. You still gotta pay rent. (*Takes a swipe at the desk with her rag, examines her work.*) Spic and span. (*Exits.*)

Episode One

At rise: **Arthur** *and* **Edmond** *are in the office.*

Art The Metaphysical Restaurant.

Ed Yes?

Art You pick up the menu: 'Idea of Ham', $8.50; 'Conception of Veal', $6.85 . . . 'Preconception of Veal,' $12.00 (eh?) . . . 'Thoughts of Asparagus' $3.50. Low overhead . . . dietetic . . . but *my* question.

Ed Yes?

Art *My* question . . .

Ed Yes?

Art Is what do you do when they want you to hold the potatoes?

Ed What do you do?

Art That is the question.

Ed (The metaphysical restaurant.)

Art It's just an idea really.

Ed Um.

Art You can't hold an imaginary potato.

Ed Um.

Art Not the best day you were born.

Ed No.

Art You can hold it in your *mind* . . .

Ed Yes.

Art But that's about it. (**Art** *crumples wrappings from foodstuffs.*) Enough lovemaking. (*Hands them to* **Ed**.) Throw this junk out, will you? Now, where were we?

Ed At the man.

Art Ah, yes. The man.

Ed Yes.

Art Here it comes. The man . . .

Ed Yes?

Art Now, the man . . . the man is in the park . . .

Ed (*transcribing*) I've got it . . .

Art He is sitting in the park regarding squirrels.

Ed Yes.

Art He sits down on a bench . . .

Ed Uh huh.

Art He clucks and a squirrel comes over. He has nothing to feed it.

Ed Mmmmmm.

Art He moves to stroke the squirrel and the squirrel bites his hand. With his other hand he grabs the squirrel and squeezes it until the creature dies. (*Pause.*) Eh?

Art Yes?

Art What do you think?

Ed What does it mean?

Art To me, or in general?

Ed Either.

Art Well, I don't know.

Ed Mmmm.

Art I'm not sure at this point.

Ed (*pause*) It's gutsy, Arthur.

Art Mmmm.

Ed It's very gutsy.

Art Thank you.

Ed Perhaps overly gutsy.

Art Mmm.

Ed And awfully short.

Art You think perhaps a greater length would temper its guts?

Ed Are you asking facetiously?

Art Not at all.

Ed Mmmm.

Art Why do you ask?

Ed For my own information.

Art Ahhhh.

Ed Could I read you something?

Art Not while we're working.

Ed What happens to the fellow?

Art I don't know.

Ed Does he die?

Art From a squirrel bite?

Ed Not necessarily.

Art Not necessarily.

Ed Not from the bite, then.

Art Then yes, he does.

Ed Um. Um. Perhaps . . . having nothing to give the squirrel, he shouldn't have clucked.

Art There needn't be a moral.

Ed No?

Art Heck no. One writes what one feels.

Ed Yes. Um. Um. What does the squirrel represent?

Art The squirrel?

Ed Yes.

Art I do not know.

Ed (A potentially non-representational animal).

Art How about this . . .

Ed (Provocative)

Art A man is walking in the park amongst (or among) the squirrels . . .

Ed Yes . . .

Art (You're doing quite well by the way.)

Ed Thank you.

Art He sees a fellow running. Chased by another fellow.

Ed . . . yes.

Art The fellow chasing shouts 'Stop that man! (Aha.) The man walking stops and considers. 'Should I try to stop that man? What is the identity of the fellow chasing the other fellow? By what authority does he ask me that I stop the guy? The *other* fellow, what would *he* request, if given the opportunity? (I wonder where they went to school, etc.) On which note he sits on a convenient bench.

Ed Yes.

Art On another end of which is perched . . . you guessed it . . . a squirrel.

Ed (*pause*) And then?

Art What?

Ed And then what?

Art (*pause*) And then.

Ed Yes?

Art He goes over to the squirrel . . .

Ed Has he anything to feed it?

Art . . . No.

Ed I think we've done that one.

Art Not quite so quickly. He goes over to the squirrel, (having nothing to feed it) and sits on its portion of the bench. He is about to initiate some action when he is arrested by shouts coming from down-path (or from down 'the' path). The shouts (and pay attention here) come from the very two men who have just run past. They are fighting. They are fighting *with each other* . . . about something . . . or other. (*Pause.*) Which took place previously. (*Pause.*) And who can blame them? Well, what do you think?

Ed . . . well . . .

Art Well, toss it out then. We'll not be hidebound by convention, eh? We start afresh. We search for guts. A simple man (which is to say, a man not heretofor invested with qualities) goes to the park to feed a squirrel. Wait. A man goes to the park to feed squirrels. (*Pause.*) A man accustomed to feeding squirrels finds himself one day in the park. (*Pause.*) Into a park usually inhabited by squirrels there came one day a man. (*Pause.*) The park! Scene of human violence and animal hunger!

Ed How about this . . .

Art Wait! I have it. Three men and a squirrel were in the park.

Ed Umm.

Art For the purpose of simplicity (and pay attention here) we can divide these four figures into two distinctive units.

Ed Umm.

Art One unit can consist of two men. They can be seen to have had some previous intercourse. Eh?

Ed Yes.

Art I mean, they run through the park, one is chasing the other, I mean, what are you going to think eh?

Ed Yes.

Art Alright. So. The second unit shall consist of the remaining man and the squirrel. Now. One man is chasing another. One man is sitting near a squirrel. One man is running down a path presumably being pursued by the initial man who is saying 'Stop that man' (his remarks being most probably addressed to the man who is sitting near the squirrel) and one squirrel is perched on a bench minding what appears to be its own business.

Ed One man and a squirrel sitting on a bench. Two men run by, the initial man being presumably chased by a second man calling 'Stop that man' . . .

Art I'm referring to the fellow giving pursuit as 'the initial man.'

Ed Oh, I'm sorry.

Art No, no. Quite alright.

Ed You're sure?

Art Yes. Absolutely. Now watch. The shouts of the two men (the initial man and his opposite number) draw the attention of the man on the bench from the squirrel which (for reasons best known to himself) he has been observing.

Ed Umm.

Art The squirrel becomes frightened and runs . . . off. Now. Before the gaze of the man on the bench can return to the bench, the space previously taken by the squirrel has been occupied BY ANOTHER SQUIRREL!

Ed (*pause*) There were three men and two squirrels in the park . . .

Art Wait, wait, wait! It will not do. It will not do. The introduction of the second animal is a mistake.

Ed Yes?

Art What do you mean, 'Yes?' Yes, of course it is. (*Pause.*) Well, think about it.

Ed (*pause*) Yes, I see your point.

Art No wait, you're wrong. Now watch. A man incapable of distinguishing between squirrels goes to the park.

The **Cleaning Woman** *enters.*

Cleaning Woman (*to* **Ed**) You wanna beer?

Art No thank you, no.

Cleaning Woman (*to* **Ed**) You, you wanna beer?

Ed No thank you.

Cleaning Woman Who's the guy?

Art My new colleague.

Cleaning Woman Oh, yeah?

Art Yes.

Cleaning Woman You doing any good?

Ed Just fine.

Cleaning Woman Aha!

Ed And you?

Cleaning Woman An, the usual stuff. Cleaning up shit . . . being lovable, the same old stuff.

Ed Um.

Cleaning Woman You wanna hear one?

Ed One what?

Cleaning Woman Well, listen, you'll find out. Here goes. (*Glances at pad.*) 'What's sauce for the *goose* . . .

Ed Yes?

Cleaning Woman . . . is the moss for the moose.' Huh?

Art Very insightful.

Cleaning Woman I just made that up in the hall.

Ed Mmmm.

Cleaning Woman So here's your content. Somebody says to his wife, 'I don't want you having sexual intercourse with anyone except me,' (*To* **Ed**.) I'm not going to offend you, am I?

Ed I don't think so.

Cleaning Woman So, the next day she comes home from the track and what do you think, he's balling her sister. (this is a true story by the way, this actually happened to me.) So she says, 'What the fuckin' piss are you doing?' and Fred says 'I'm balling your sister.' To which one could reply. 'What's sauce for the goose is moss for the moose.' (*Pause.*) It's a variation on a theme. You been around the block. You know the actual old saying, 'What's sauce for the goose is . . . uh . . . sauce for the gander.' But let me ask you something.

Ed Alright.

Cleaning Woman When was the last time you heard that saying used? (*Pause.*) And you know why? Because it has no meaning in today's society.

Ed Yes.

Cleaning Woman Well, what the hey, times change. There's no use crying over spilt milk.

Ed Yes.

Cleaning Woman I mean, you stop to think about it, there's no use crying over any kind of milk.

Ed No.

Cleaning Woman It's a senseless act.

Ed Yes.

Cleaning Woman It's the act of a neurotic personality.

Ed Yes.

Cleaning Woman It's the act of a madman.

Ed Ummm.

Cleaning Woman It's a topsy-turvy anything-can-happen world.

Ed Um.

Cleaning Woman And we're all a hell of a lot better off without it. (*Consults pad.*) Hey! So listen to this. There's these two guys, right, the Kid and Black Bart, vicious enemies. So the kid says 'Slap leather, Bart' and Bart says, 'Kid the man can beat me to the draw ain't been born yet, and the man don't live who ain't been born yet.' Kid says, 'Enough fucking rhetoric, huh, go for your gun you're getting old.' Bart says, 'Who isn't?' They think about this awhile. Sun sets. Kid says, 'Bar' says, 'What the heck, huh, I got some spare pork and beans over to the campfire, come on over, we'll talk it out, maybe we can settle this thing amicably.' Bart says, 'Kid,' says 'Kid, you got yourself a deal.' They go over to the campfire. So there's the campfire. Fucking campfire is full of sidekicks. Basically, they're Mexican or of Mexican extraction. Everybody's wrapped in their blanket. Colder than a witch's tit. Guys say, 'What are you doing with Black Bart, kid?' Kid says, 'We're going to sit down and talk it out, perhaps we can become pals.' Guys say, 'I ain't being pals with no fucking Gringo.' Kid says, 'So what do you think *I* am, Porfirio Diaz?' Fuckin' guys, recognition dawns on their faces, they all slap leather, Kid goes out in a hail of molten lead. They turn on Black Bart. 'Click, click' go their guns. (They're empty.) Bart seizes the main chance, and grabs a horse from a nearby place, gallops into the Western night, never heard from again. Five years later, the horse turns up for auction at a dog food plant in Chicago. One of the bandits (now grown up) recognizes the horse and buys him. His plan, Bart galloped off he tore part of his shirt on a nearby cactus. The guy has *saved* the shirt. He sits in the park with the horse day after day holding the shirt beneath the horse's nose and whispering 'Go get 'em, boy'. Fuckin' horse will not track. Sits in the park with a shirt under his nose. Finally they get tossed out by the cops. Who do you think one of the cops is? (*Consults pad.*)

Ed Who?

Cleaning Woman I have no idea. (*To* **Art**.) You want me to not touch anything today?

Art No.

Cleaning Woman (*To* **Ed**) So I got one for you. What does he mean?

Ed I have no idea.

Cleaning Woman Good for you. (*To* **Art**.) You want me to empty the wastebasket?

Art Is it full?

Cleaning Woman It's not exactly *full*. There are things in it. Apparently wrappings from foodstuff.

Art (Vicious cunt.)

Cleaning Woman Alright, alright. I don't like to cause friction. Friction wears you down. That's why they call it '*friction*.' I come in here every day. I do my job. What am I to you? Old. An old cleaning woman. A woman who just comes in and cleans. (*Pause.*) I was young once.

Ed Nothing so very extraordinary in that.

Cleaning Woman I like you. You're all right.

Ed Thank you.

Cleaning Woman So how'd you fall in with *this* sorry sack of shit.

Art I think that's just about enough.

Cleaning Woman I got more dialogue. (*Strikes a pose.*) I've seen a lot in my time. I been about a bit. I was married once . . .

Ed I'll bet there's a story in that.

Cleaning Woman Don't be so sure. I've had experiences. Loads of 'em: one after the other. Very personal. Must we live in a world where every individual is condemned to make the same or awfully fucking similar mistakes? Must we live in a world like that? I hope not and I like to think not.

Art (This girl can act!)

Cleaning Woman (*to audience*) I have had many experiences – professional, amateur, and imaginary – in the theatre. (*To* **Art**.) So, you want the wastebasket emptied?

Art You may empty the wastebasket.

Cleaning Woman It's all the same to me.

Art Well, just leave it full, then, if it gives you such pleasure.

Cleaning Woman I will. And I'm paid to empty it. So find the silly goose in the picture. (*Pause.*) I see no reason to stay here any longer. (*Exits.*)

Art (*pause*) That was the cleaning woman.

Ed Oh.

Art (*pause*) Well, back to work.

Ed Yes. (*Taking up pad.*)

Art Busy, busy, busy.

Ed Business.

Art No problem too large, no problem too small.

Ed No.

Art All problems just right. It was a lovely day in the park, devoid of human life. A small, nameless squirrel who called the park 'home' was gathering nuts. For the winter. When he would eat them. All up.

Ed One fall day a squirrel was in the park looking for nuts to eat later on.

Art I believe I've said that. He looked high and low for those nuts (his satisfaction in the gustation of which would – instinctively – though not outside the mainstream of traditional Protestant thought – be deferred until a later, colder time.) Winter was a'comin on. Already the trees were beginning to shrink from the hideous burden of their lifeless leaves. A morbid time. A time of violence in the face of Famine and of Cold. (*Pause.*) A time to gather nuts.

Ed (*pause*) May I try one?

Art What?

Ed I was asking, could I try one?

Art Yes, please do.

Ed (*taking stage*) Once upon a time there was a small and peaceful park, beloved of men and animals alike. A very nice place. Day and night through the warmer months men would labor over each and every flower, and each tree, shaping . . . pruning . . . applying mulch and water in those cases wherein nature had been lax.

Art Are you daft?

Ed Daft? No. Why do you ask?

Art I was asking for my own information.

Ed (*pause*) Shall I continue?

Art Well, how do you feel? Would you like to?

Ed I felt I was on to something.

Art On to what?

Ed On to some thread or essence.

Art On the basis of one paragraph?

Ed Well . . .

Art If that's what you felt, then do not let me dissuade you. (*Pause.* **Edmond** *wilts.*) Right. Well, then, enough improvisation. Enough lovemaking. Once there was a bench. No. Wait. Wait. A man comes into a park with no intention of strangling a squirrel, but does so. Two other men, each perfectly conscious of what he is up to, run through the park, one preceded by the other. And one squirrel sits on a little bench. Um . . . um . . .

Ed Uh, squirrels!

Art Yes?

Ed Gatherers of nuts.

Art Go on.

Ed Harbingers of Autumn.

Art I think not.

Ed In any case, habitants of the park.

Art I give you that.

Ed Small, fur-bearing, harmless.

Art One would hope so.

Ed Men!

Art (Men.)

Ed Omnivorous, sentient, warm-blooded.

Art Go on.

Ed THE PARK! Home to one and recreation to the

other! (*Pause.*) How long have you been working on this story?

Art Ah, time, time, time.

Ed Um.

Art So, let's just exercise a small bit of control over our horses here. A man leaving the park thinks back on the events of the afternoon. The fight he has witnessed . . . the squirrel he has strangled . . . 'What does it all mean?' he thinks to himself.

Ed And what does he respond?

Art Well, wait a second.

Ed Let me try.

Art What?

Ed Let me try.

Art I'm sorry, what?

Ed I want to try one!

Art Well, please do.

Ed An unhappy man with nothing to feed squirrels comes to the park to forget. Sitting on a bench his efforts are hampered by the presence of a squirrel.

Art Isn't it funny how people will say, 'I'm so hungry I could eat a horse' but never 'I'm so late I could *ride* a horse?'

Ed Are you hungry?

Art Not particularly.

Ed Oh. (*Pause.*) Annoyedly . . .

Art Watch your adverbs.

Ed . . . he looks at the squirrel.

Art Aha.

Ed His glance, originally filled with reproach, is softened by the mindless creature's happy behavior. (Do we spell that with, or without, a 'u'?)

Art Without.

Ed Alright. Forgetting his lack of comestibles, he clucks.

Art (I bet.)

Ed The squirrel approaches. The man moves to stroke the squirrel . . . And the squirrel – startled by far-off cries – bites the man – hard. Not wishing to appear a fool, the man begins to choke the creature until the squirrel, in a death-*like* state, releases its grip. The man then leaves the park to staunch his wound and continue in his efforts to forget.

Art (Or I'm so sensitive I could *draw* a horse.)

Ed Oblivious to the cries of two dishevelled gents mixing it up nearby, the squirrel struggles back to consciousness, forces air into its broken lungs, and hops painfully back to its nest in a nearby tree. The next day . . .

Art (Or I'm so petty I could mistreat a horse.)

Ed Mmmm.

Art (Let's face the facts.)

Ed Its mind full of mute revenge, the squirrel returns to the bench, as does the man. *And the process is repeated*!

Art Say, you know, I *am* a little hungry.

Ed Oh.

Art So, tell me, Edward, what have you brought for lunch today?

Ed *Edmond*.

Art So, tell me, Edmond, what have *you* brought for lunch today?

Ed Well, I've brought myself a sandwich and some milk.

Art Milk!

Ed Yes.

Art Ah, milk.

Ed Um.

Art I *like* to drink milk.

Ed So do I.

Art I like the way it looks.

Ed Uh huh.

Art *And* I like the way it tastes.

Ed Silly to drink it otherwise.

Art I've always thought so.

Ed (*pause*) Would you like some milk?

Art Why, yes, I would.

Ed *hands* **Art** *carton of milk.*

Art Hideous substance when you come to think of it.

Ed Um. (*Takes out sandwich and raises it to his mouth.*)

Art Roastbeef! Is that roastbeef?

Ed Yes.

Art (*staring at sandwich*) I *knew* it! I just knew it.

Ed Would you like some?

Art Would I *like* some?

Ed Yes.

Art Why, yes! (**Art** *takes the whole sandwich, opens it, looks inside.*) Well, well, if it isn't my younger brother just returned from college. (*Takes a bite.*) So, it seems that what we have today is squirrels.

Ed Squirrels.

Art *Filthy* beggars.

Ed Um.

Art But nonetheless, a squirrel comes into the park.

Ed Um.

Art Best place in the world for 'em. (*To* **Ed**.) Have you got a cupcake?

Ed *shakes head.*

Art He has some sort of relationship with a man. We follow the two before, during, and after their fateful meeting. Whence they came, what they did, whither they went. Beginning, middle, end. At any point squirrel, or (or 'and/or') man, can be described as being closer to or farther from point A (inception) than (or to) point B (conclusion). Dynamism. Plot. Character. Human longing. The life of the soul expressed through Art. Nothing less.

Ed Um.

Art Man meets squirrel. Squirrel bites man. Man kills squirrel. From nothing, *to* nothing. Watch now. 'Nothing,' rising action. Climax. Falling action. 'Nothing.' Eh? We always clean up when we're done. So, what have we today, eh, Edmond? A man (some man, some unknown creature, some receptacle of the godhead) goes into the park. He sits on a bench by that furry, grey creature, the Squirrel.

Ed The *grey* squirrel.

Art He has nothing to feed it. (God.) He clucks and a squirrel comes over. He moves to pet the squirrel, and the squirrel bites his hand. With his other hand he grabs the squirrel and squeezes it until the squirrel dies. Eh? Eh?

Ed May I ask a question?

Art That's what you're here for.

Ed What does this mean?

Art Meaning? Meaning?

Ed Yes.

Art Ah, meaning! Meaning meaning meaning meaning meaning. Meaning meaning meaning. You ask me about meaning and I respond with gibberish. What kind of a friend am I? Are you sure you don't have a cupcake?

Ed No.

Art Let me tell you something, Edmond. And if you never hear another thing in your life, remember this. Art is art.

Ed (*pause*) You know, I feel that, strictly speaking, that is not quite true.

Art Art is not art? (*Pause.*) Then what is art? (*Pause.*) Think about it. I've got to pee. (*Delivers from the door.*) And while he was away the elves came and filled the blank pages with deathless prose. He read them one by one on his return, his heart full, his bladder empty. 'What elves!' he thought. 'Tonight I shall make them shoes.' (*Exits.*)

Edmond *jumps up, grabs cupcake from lunchbag, and stuffs it into his mouth, as* **Cleaning Woman** *enters.*

Cleaning Woman You wanna' make love?

Ed Well, no. I don't think so, no.

Cleaning Woman That's all right. So how are you doing?

Ed I'm doing fine. (*Pause.*) How you doing?

Cleaning Woman How should I do? I go around, I got my tools, my mop and my rag, I hum a bit. I listen to the radio in offices where it's applicable. Weather means very little as I work inside. Very few variables. I have a lot of time to myself. (*Consults pad.*) Sit down in that chair. (**Ed** *sits.*) So. Lookit here. (*Refers to pad occasionally during this speech.*) The future! Planet XZ 84773. Fourth world in the Goolagong System. Poisonous atmosphere of Clorox. On

the surface, weird shit all over the place. A spaceship.
Blasting through the thickened mist. Slowing, settling,
down into the murk, CHUNK. It has settled. A long
pause. (We'll just indicate it.) Who can tell how long in
the thickened time and timelessness of this once mighty
world. Ah, Time, Time! Time, you old albatross.
(Although it is, of course, a little precious to speak of time
as being 'old,' huh?).

Ed Um.

Cleaning Woman You *young* albatross. Time! Rushing to
your logical conclusion. (*Pause.*) Do you like Science
Fiction?

Ed Not particularly.

Cleaning Woman Oh. So you going to stick it out here?

Ed I think so, yes.

Cleaning Woman Well, you're working without a net,
Bud. Your partner is just jerking himself off, artistically
speaking, and has been for years. That's right. We were a
number once (though you wouldn't believe it to look at
him). But the cat is dead and dried and hung in the
freezer of forgotten dreams. And if you got any sense,
you'll hit the fuckin' highway quicker than it takes to tell.

Art (*OSV*) Meanwhile, poised above the porcelain pissoir,
our hero.

Cleaning Woman Oops.

Art What fantasies, what strange and improbable
machinations of fate coursing through his mind. (The
distraught mind is not the worst creator.) (Neither is it the
best creator.) (It is, perhaps, a creator of variable value.)
(Depending, of course, on that which is to be created.)
(Among other things.) He finishes. Whips the last
lingering drops from his dick, buttons his fly, and
proceeds back to the office. 'Plack, plack' go his feet on the
marble. 'Good to be getting back to work.' Approaching

the office door he hears strange cries within. Cries of pain, of anguish, of the fear of death. Cries of his brand new partner in the clutches of malfaction. An inchoate animal warning buzzes in his brain. 'You've forgotten to wash your hands!' Back he goes . . .

Cleaning Woman (*A short reprieve.*)

Ed Have you worked here long?

Cleaning Woman Long enough to know better, let me tell you. You know what, everybody talks about the weather, but nobody ever does anything about it, you know? Except *him*. He never talks about the weather. You wanna' make love? (I asked you that.) That's okay.

Ed Would you like to read something? (*Picks up briefcase.*)

Cleaning Woman Sure.

They are looking at **Edmond**'s *work, as* **Arthur** *enters.*

Art What were you doing?

Cleaning Woman Cleaning the office.

Art You've already cleaned it once today.

Cleaning Woman You got a mind like an elephant, you know that?

Art Um.

Cleaning Woman And the soul of a pawnbroker. You got the soul of some 19th Century Russian pawnbroker and her sister.

Art Are you still working on that Civil War thing?

Cleaning Woman What can you say about the Civil War? Woman writes Uncle Tom's Cabin, Lincoln frees slaves, country splits in two, fights for four years, North wins. Big deal. And, if it happens to decide to appear in print, I hope it remembers who wrote it. And I don't think I'm casting aspersions about the professional honesty of any persons present that just might catch the

ears of one not acquainted with certain people's past
history and be unduly influenced by it.

Art (*pause*) You know, sometimes I feel that you exceed
the presecribed bounds of your operations.

Cleaning Woman Well, you could be right.

Art I feel I *am* right.

Cleaning Woman Well, can I tell you something?

Art Yes, please do.

Cleaning Woman Nothing is more important than that.
(*Exits.*)

Art Well, where were we?

Interlude One

At rise: *It is night time. The* **Cleaning Woman** *is alone in the
office, creating.*

Cleaning Woman The moon. The moon*light*. Shining on
the ocean right before their tent. Behind them the desert.
Sand. (And a hell of a trip.) Before them the water and
another trip. And there they were on the goddamned
edge. Between two emptinesses. (huh) Between fatigue
and resolution. Between effort and effort. On the beach.
(*Examines what she's written. Tosses it in wastebasket.*) They
wore themselves out in the desert. They sat in their tent in
the moonlight and looked at the ocean they would have to
cross. They listened to the waves, and the monotonous
rhythm of the waves put them to sleep. (*Makes a correction
on her pad.*) They listened to the waves and the waves put
them to sleep. (*Examines what she's written. Tosses it in
wastebasket.*) They crossed the desert. They had to cross
the ocean. They sat in their tent and thought about their
effort. (*Scratches it out and corrects what she's written.*) They
crossed the desert. They had to cross the ocean. They sat
in their tent and didn't think about anything. (*Examines*

what she's written. Tosses it out.) They sat in their fuckin' tent in the moonlight. (*Pause.*) And listened to the waves. (*Pause.*) And fell asleep. (*Examines what she's written.*) They sat in their tent in the moonlight. And listened to the waves. And fell asleep. (*Pause.*) (*Tucks paper in her pocket.*) You make your own fun.

Episode Two

At rise: **Arthur** *and* **Edmond** *are in the office collaborating.*

Ed Toy boat.

Art Yes.

Ed Toy boat, toy boat, toy boat, toy boat, toy boat.

Art You're doing fine.

Ed The words, in effect, *become* our toyboat.

Art How about this . . .

Ed *Real* boat.

Art . . . a man is sitting in the park amongst the squirrels . . .

Ed We've done that one.

Art Not quite so quickly. He sits on a bench. He clucks. Over comes a squirrel looking for food. The man has no food, because of rising grocery costs. The squirrel cannot understand this, and the man . . . out of pity for the poor thing's mindless state – moves to stroke the squirrel.

Ed Toy *and* real boat.

Art The squirrel . . . never having been able to interpret affectionate overtures correctly (and the reason for this is: perhaps, material for a whole *new* story) bites the man and the man, having his first compassionate action in years rebuffed, *kills* the squirrel. (*Pause.*) Or words to that effect.

Ed Throughout that long first year of the war Susan and Terry lived in warmth and comfort in the small apartment overlooking the park.

Art You're digging your own grave.

Ed Strolling through the park one day, he noticed her by the fountain.

Art I'll be damned if I don't wonder what we have for lunch today.

Ed Perhaps it was the breeze wafting a trace of her perfume . . . perhaps she was hailing him . . .

Art Perhaps he was looking for her. Maybe it was his sister. These things happen.

Ed All of a sudden it was like the first time all over again. It was as if it were the first time. (*Pause.*) It *was* the first time. 'You're new here.' he said. Slowly her eyes raised to meet his. (He was taller than she.) But her gaze was drawn over his shoulder . . . over his incredibly low shoulder . . . to . . . a scene of unspeakable terror . . . which she promptly ignored.

Art Wait a second! This is happening in the park?

Ed Yes.

Art Hmmm. Good use of space. Man and woman meeting in park. Raises eyes . . . looks over shoulder, ignores terror . . . perhaps glimpses squirrel . . . interesting. Day after day she saw him on his solitary ambles through the park. Though confined to a wheelchair, her vision was of the best. (*Pause.*) Though dependent on crutches she could see quite well. (*Pause.*) She was nearsighted, and she limped, but neither served to diminish her enjoyment of an afternoon with nature. The two combatants, the funny old man on the bench . . . the little squirrel (which, being French, she could not help but think of as 'le petit Ventregris,' or alternatively, '*la* petite equerelle') . . .

Ed Bateau veritable.

Art Pay attention. Day after day she saw him. 'What is he thinking of?' she wondered. 'Does he ever think of me? What will become of me? How will I meet the vicissitudes of the coming winter? Will I find happiness and fulfilment in love? In a new job? Is there more to life than popularity? Does Joe really think I'm pretty or does he just *say* so, cause he knows that's why I let him fuck me?' (*Pause.*) Suddenly, her gaze was drawn . . .

Ed We've done that one.

Art Suddenly her look was attracted to a small squirrel sorting through the leaves not three feet from her. Having fixed her gaze on the creature (not without difficulty), she was struck by its industry. Its healthy fur and bright black eyes. But wait! Around its neck . . . yes! Circling its neck . . . a large red welt. As if it had been strangled! Incompletely strangled! (*Pause.*) Day after day! (*Pause.*) By an old man!

Ed Arthur . . .

Art No. I'm hot! I'm hot! And as she stood, musing on the injustice of a system which permits a mindless animal (even one so hideously deformed) to acquire sustenance through looking under leaves, while compelling her to labor in a . . .

Ed Do it later.

Art Even as she so mused . . . tears running down her cheeks . . . tears running *up* and down her cheeks . . . blood congealing on her ankle where the brace had chafed it raw. (now that really is a bit much) But nonetheless, where was I . . . uh . . .

Ed I've got it! The sky darkened, the rain began to fall. (*Pause.*) Down. 'Oh no,' she thought. 'It's raining.' (Hurries through park to street.)

Art Out of park?

Ed Wait. She stepped off the curb in the low thick rain
and into the path of an onrushing schoolbus . . . the driver
trying desperately to see, and not being aided any by the
windshield wipers swishing so *constantly*, now one way,
now another . . . What was that? A small, rather
European looking woman in glasses standing inevitably in
the path of the bus. 'HONK HONK,' went the horn. (The
children, unaware of the drama through which they were
being borne, continued to natter of recess and soap-
sculpture.)

Art (I bet.)

Ed Back on the curb she stepped. Her heart pounding
fast. Faster. Tooo fast! The world began to swim before
her eyes. She saw spots! She saw stars! She saw the whole
interdigitating mishmosh revealed in its total complexity,
before lapsing – not without regret – into the final state
from which there is no furlough. (*Pause.*) And then she
woke up.

Art I don't like it.

Ed Why not?

Art Too faggy. (*Pause.*) Are you feeling well today?

Ed Yes, why do you ask?

Art Well, you're looking well, I thought I'd ask if you
were feeling well.

Ed Mmmm. Quite well, thanks.

Art You know, every job has its rhythms.

Ed I'm aware of that.

Art I know you are.

Ed I think I will enjoy my work here.

Art Mmm.

Ed And not just for the reasons that you think.

Art No?

Ed I think not, no.

Art What reasons, then?

Ed Different ones.

Art What reasons do you think I think?

Ed You think my reasons might be incorrect?

Art Do I?

Ed Yes.

Art Well, yes, I do.

Ed You see!

Art I do.

Ed That's what I thought.

Art I know you did.

Ed I *do*.

Art I know you do.

Ed I think I know that.

Art Do you?

Ed Yes, I think I do.

Art You do?

Ed I think so.

Art So do I.

Ed You do?

Art I do.

Ed (*pause*) Do what? (*Pause.*) DO WHAT?

Art (*pause*) Do you ever think of yourself as a pederast?

Ed No. (*Pause.*) Do you?

Art From time to time.

Ed And why is that?

Art Because it's such a beautiful word. (*Pause.*) Yes. The Squirrel!

Ed Oh.

Art A series of embarrassingly personal, thinly-veiled glimpses into the life of a true rodent. A surreal but somehow touching account of the day-to-day realities of a workaday squirrel. Curtain going aside. A well-lit parlor. A fire in the grate. Hunting prints. In the center of the table, one incredibly small armchair. (*Pause.*) Suddenly . . . (*Pause.*)

Ed Yes?

Art *She* was there!

Ed Again?

Art Fresh from a day in the park. Her face a bunch of contradictory impressions. Her figure incredibly je ne sais quoi. Her well-turned ankles. Her nicotene-stained . . . fingers. The huge bull mastiff at her side, restrained by a simple strand of . . . (*Pause.*) Out she went. Then, a knock at the door. Silence. The knock is repeated . . . The door opens . . . (*Pause.*)

Ed Who is there?

Art Formalist. Formal formal formalist!

Ed It's just a word.

Art And not one to be proud of. Have you learned nothing working here?

Ed No.

Art And what is that supposed to mean?

Ed What would you like it to mean?

Art 'What would I like it to mean.' Indeed. There's more than one fish in the sea.

Ed I don't quite see how that applies.

Art Think about it.

Ed I shall.

Art I'll just bet you shall. (*Pause.*) Edmond. Edmond. Ed. Eddy. Let's not have friction. Friction wears one down. (*Pause.*) You know that. We have a job to do here, and our job is to do it. Eh? Eh? (*Pause.*) Looky here. Now just take up your pencil now and here we go. Now aren't you happy here? Mmmm? Mmmm? I know you are. These fights are nothing more than that. Isn't that so? Of course it is. You're very good for me. You know that we work well, together, you know that, Eh? Eh? (*Pause.*) Suuure. (*Pause.*) Come on now. (*Throughout speech,* **Art** *has been trying to wedge a pencil between* **Edmond**'s *fingers. He finally succeeds.*) That's better. Yes. I'm sorry for what I said.

Ed I've forgotten all about it.

Art I know you have, and so have I. So here. The squirrel lay in the shade of a big tree root.

Ed (Restful.)

Art Playing oppossum. A crowded day in the park. People running. People sitting on benches. The benches themselves. Animals foraging for food, or merely passing time between the sun and sun.

Ed A man must come to grips with artiface.

Art Clouds wafting overhead . . . soil stable underfoot. The friendly cop on the beat . . . uh . . .

The **Cleaning Woman** *enters.*

Cleaning Woman Anybody up for making love?

Art I think not, no.

Cleaning Woman (*to* **Ed**) You?

Ed *shakes head.*

Cleaning Woman I know, you're busy.

Art We're not busy, we're just sitting here without a care in the whole wide world and being cruel.

Cleaning Woman Whatever gets you off.

Art Haven't you offices to clean?

Cleaning Woman You bet your ass, and that's why they call me the cleaning woman. (They're no fools.) (*To* **Ed**.) So, how you getting on?

Ed We're getting on just fine.

Cleaning Woman I'm glad to hear it. (And this from a woman who's here all night every night and many times 'til dawn cleaning the offices and generally making herself available.) (*Pause.*) Well, stuff to do, places to go, floors to mop. (*Exits.*)

Art (*pause*) She was an old woman. Stooped from years of scrubbing. Degenerate. Licentious. Her filthy hands were . . . nah, fuck her. She was young and healthy. Dressed in a simple something-or-other for a nice day in the park . . . uh . . .

Ed 'Boo hoo,' went the little children, huddled around the space heater. 'Isn't Daddy coming home tonight?'

Art 'Isn't Daddy coming home tonight?' asked the little children. *Then*, 'Boo hoo.'

Ed Ah, yes.

Art You bet your ass. She was young and healthy. Dressed in a simple woolen robe.

Ed (Itchy.)

Art After a filling day in the park. And not too concerned about the broken furnace. All in all, it was a sort of adventure for her and the kiddies. The high snow had probably kept their father late. 'Isn't Daddy coming home tonight?' asked the children. 'Is he dead, Mom?'

Ed 'Oh, dear' she thought. 'I do hope he was able to see the doctor about his bitten hand.'

Art Don't try to placate me. (*Pause.*) And so engrossed in thought she was, she did not hear the 'Pad Pad Pad' of Rusty, their prize Doberman, on the parquet behind her. She had forgotten to feed him for the last three weeks running, and from the corner of his jaws hung a red-stained rag of someone's Doctor Denton. 'Bark bark' went the dog. (*Pause.*) Isn't that just like a dog?

Interlude Two

At rise: **Edmond** *and the* **Cleaning Woman** *are alone in the office. It is late at night.*

Cleaning Woman '. . . slowly her eyes raised to meet his. "But I will *drown*," she said. "That, my dear," he retorted, "is just about what I had in mind." ' (*Pause.*) Strike out everything from 'That, my dear,' and insert 'Ha ha ha.' You wanna beer?

Ed *shakes head.*

Cleaning Woman Chapter Two.

Ed Are we using Roman or Arabic numerals for the chapters?

Cleaning Woman What did we do on the first one?

Ed (*looks*) We wrote it out.

Cleaning Woman We'll use Roman numerals on this one, then.

Ed Right.

Cleaning Woman Chapter Two, A Tale of the Cross. Ready? (**Ed** *nods.*) 'Bubbles. Bubbles bubbles bubbles.

Floating ever-upward. Ever toward the surface. Toward
the light. Pretty bubbles full of air. Rising to the heaven of
an open sky.' (huh?) (*Pause.*) 'Chains. chains chains
chains. Chains of lead. Dragging. Dragging her ever
downward. Down through the water to a gooey grave.'
(*Pause.*) 'Hope. Hope hope hope. Springing eternal in the
human breast . . . uh . . .

Ed (*pause*) Would you like to go back to work on the Civil
War thing?

Cleaning Woman The what?

Ed That piece about the Civil War.

Cleaning Woman Where'd you hear about that?

Ed Well, you were working on one with Arthur, weren't
you?

Cleaning Woman That? Oh, *that*. The north-south
number.

Ed Yes.

Cleaning Woman Well, it seems a shame. I mean we
already got a running start on this one.

Ed Yes . . .

Cleaning Woman I mean, you're working on a thing you
should continue to work on it until you're done or
something stops you. I don't know. Just when it seems
you're on to something, all of a sudden, 'Boof,' and what's
happening, huh? Shit, I still got two more suites and the
hall to do.

Ed Well, let's just try it for a little while . . .

Cleaning Woman Well . . .

Ed And if you needed . . . or wanted . . . some help, later,
with your offices, or the hall, perhaps I could . . . (that is,
I would be happy to) help you out a bit.

Cleaning Woman A real offer, huh?

Ed You bet.

Cleaning Woman (*pause*) Nah. Forget it. Takes no time at all. But thanks for asking.

Ed You sure now?

Cleaning Woman Oh, yeah. (*Pause.*) You working today?

Ed *nods head.*

Cleaning Woman So, go and get some rest. Go on. I'll see you later. (**Ed** *picks up briefcase and starts to leave.*) Hey hey wait. Hey, what about that junk of yours you wanted me to read? You got it?

Ed (*clutching briefcase behind his back*) No. I haven't got it with me.

Cleaning Woman That's okay. You bring it in, I'll read it, huh?

Ed You bet.

Cleaning Woman Okay, okay, okay . . . goodnight.

Ed Goodnight. (*Exits.*)

Cleaning Woman Okay. (*Pause.*) So she says, 'Smoke your *own* salmon, then talk. Cultivate your *own* garden, *then* talk. (Always some preliminary to speech.) He misinterprets her. Thinks she's driving him away. It's been known to happen. He joins the Royal Canadian Mounted Police. Finds out the horses are only for show. Defects. There he is, up in the Bering Straits. Russia just a few blocks away, all frozen over. He looks back. Sled dogs! The famous sled dogs of the Royal Canadian Mounted Police . . . The lead dog spots him. 'Woof woof,' goes the dog. (Just like a dog.) Out onto the ice he goes. Mother Russia closer and closer. CRAAAAAK. He looks down, this incredible chasm is opening between his feet. He jumps to the left. Plop! through the ice he goes. Finds himself staring at a walrus. Recognizes it instantly. Gets the hell out of *there*. Jumps back on the floe. Cops wait on

the shore. Figure he's going to freeze solid, they'll bring
him in with tongs. Starts for Russia. One arm freezes. One
leg. Other arm. BAM! A frozen statue. Blood starts to
freeze. His last thought, he thinks of me. His heart pumps
faster. His crotch gets hot. His armpits. His lymph nodes.
Water flows off him like a duck's back. He is steaming. He
is horny. He is free. He rushes onto Mother Russia a free
man and gives the Mounties the finger. They give him the
finger. He gives them the finger. They give him the finger.
Five months later, the rescue party finds everybody dead
from starvation, middle fingers on their right hand
pointing 'cross the Bering Strait. (*Pause.*) So what is the
price of animosity?

Episode Three

At rise: **Arthur** *and* **Edmond** *are collaborating.*

Art Shit. Shit shit shit shit shit. My pencil is broken. A
broken pencil. Eh? The most high-flown plans . . . words
of import . . . thoughts of importance. I'm having them.
In my head. And they're staying there because of a simple
mechanical malfunction. A simple weakness of wood or
graphite. A simple exertion of a pressure on the
instrument perhaps greater than that for which it was
designed. Can you beat this? Can you beat this with a
large stick? I think not. (*Pause.*) How is the pencil
sharpener working?

Ed (*tries it*) Seems to be operating perfectly.

Art And there's the rub, one instrument functioning
impeccably and the other shattered beyond hope of repair.
Eh? I am in the midst of a sentence, the pencil sharpener
is operating perfectly, and the *pencil* breaks!

Ed You're probably overwrought.

Art Shit. Take this down. It was a brisk and bracing day
out in the park . . .

Ed Just 'brisk' I think.

Art It was a brisk day in the park. Pigeons wheeling overhead.The scent of . . . blank . . . wafting from the . . . (*Looks at* **Ed**.)

Ed Well, to a large extent it depends on the scent.

Art There was an indefinable scent wafting. They were meeting in the park. For the last time. 'Well,' he thought. 'All things have their limit.' 'Fish and visitors begin to stink after three days. Even the best of fish. (Though they, being dead, are mercifully inured to their own putrescence.) (As is the case with visitors, the stink being only figurative.) (As is the case with shit – not being sentient.)' Ah, Love Love Love. It makes the world go 'round. It makes those same revolutions bearable. (*Pause.*) And it leads us to philosophise on the process, too! What did she see in him, anyway. Huh? (*Pause.*) Does it ever seem to you that you're losing your ability to generalize?

Ed Tell it to the Marines.

Art I disapprove of the Marines.

Ed Then tell it to the Small Business Administration.

Art Are you feeling alright today?

Ed Quite well, thank you.

Art Yes. Ah, Time Time Time. You old pee-pee head. (*Pause.*) The people yearn for poetry. It's a thankless job.

Ed But not without its compensations.

Art The terror of an empty sheet of Foolscap. (*Pause.*) The joy of sexual fulfillment. (*Pause.*) The embarrassment of fecal incontinence. (*Pause.*) Words Words Words. The fluid . . . flow of words. One right after the other. (*Pause.*) Isn't it strange that it is acceptable in polite usage to refer to a witch's tit only for purposes of comparison . . . go to any social gathering and remark that the weather is as cold as a witch's tit and no one bats an eye. Ask. 'What do you *think* of a witch's tit', and you're branded as a boor.

Ed I've got to pee. (*Exits.*)

Enter the **Cleaning Woman**.

Art Does it ever seem to you that you're losing your ability to generalize?

Cleaning Woman Talent isn't everything.

Art Now wherever did you hear that?

Cleaning Woman You still got your old way with an adjective.

Art There's more to life than a facility with modifiers. It's possible that I've lost the touch. (*Pause.*) Once broken, never mended.

Cleaning Woman You think so?

Art Look at the case of the hymen.

Cleaning Woman The way I see it, it's never too late. (*Pause.*) And on the other hand, tough tit. So, how's your pal?

Art Him? He's not my pal.

Cleaning Woman He's not?

Art My pal was kidnapped weeks ago by Martians. He is a cunning imitation sent from Mars to torment and corrupt me.

Cleaning Woman You don't tell me.

Art I'm afraid I do.

Cleaning Woman So how'd you find out this?

Art He has malfunctioned and is behaving erratically.

Cleaning Woman Oh, yeah?

Art I hope to tell you.

Cleaning Woman (*pause*) You got any junk around here you'd like me to clean up?

Art No.

Cleaning Woman Okay. (*Starts to go.*)

Art Do you remember that afternoon in the park?

Cleaning Woman When?

Art Long, long ago.

Cleaning Woman Long ago?

Art Afternoon in park. Sun. Grass. (Perhaps a squirrel.) Trees . . . She was there.

Cleaning Woman How we loved her.

Art We were young then.

Cleaning Woman We're still young.

Art Life was not complex.

Cleaning Woman You got by rhyming 'mustard' and 'custard.'

Art Nothing mattered.

Cleaning Woman You could still get it up artistically.

Art She was there.

Cleaning Woman She was still there?

Art In the time of which I am speaking, yes.

Cleaning Woman And suddenly . . . (*Looks at* **Art**.) or . . . gradually . . . the hell with it. *You* tell the story.

Art And suddenly (in the fullness of time) everything had taken on a new meaning. And lost the old meaning. The sun overhead. The cracks in the pavement underfoot (the source of much maternal discomfort) The benches . . . the trees . . . many other objects made of wood.

Cleaning Woman How full of life we were.

Art How full of promise.

Cleaning Woman How lovely she was then.

Art How young.

Cleaning Woman *How* young?

Art A mere fifteen.

Cleaning Woman Enticing jailbait.

Art How sweet her lips.

Cleaning Woman How bright her eyes.

Art That vacant stare of hers.

Cleaning Woman She loved the movies so.

Art That child loved film.

Cleaning Woman Her honey breath.

Art Her ignorance of contraceptive technique.

Cleaning Woman 'Spank me,' she said, 'for I've been bad.'

Art The bench . . . her bench.

Cleaning Woman She loved that bench.

Art She loved to sit on it.

Cleaning Woman That shapely derrière.

Art So young . . . so full of promise.

Cleaning Woman Her face on Christmas morning.

Art Her leg on Labor Day.

Cleaning Woman The inconsistency in her treatment of service personnel . . .

Art Were we too harsh?

Cleaning Woman Who the fuck knows?

Art Ah, Time Time Time. Only the past is susceptible to

change. The future belongs to those who prepare for it. The past, to everyone.

Cleaning Woman That's not bad.

Art You really think so?

Cleaning Woman Well, I don't know. I *said* it, if that's any indication.

Art Are you baiting me?

Cleaning Woman I don't think so.

Art Well, that's what it sounds like to me.

Cleaning Woman Bite on a bullet. (*Pause.*) Lookit, couldn't we be pals?

Art I feel that I could be a 'pal.'

Cleaning Woman Well, let's be pals then.

Art I haven't had a pal since gradeschool.

Cleaning Woman Well, I will be your pal.

Art And I will be your pal.

Cleaning Woman And I will be yours.

Art I don't believe you.

Cleaning Woman Go to Paris and suffer. (*Pause.*) Well, lookit I've enjoyed this. (*Starts to go.*)

Art Wait. Wait. Flirt with me a minute, will you?

Cleaning Woman Where did you get that shirt?

Art Do you like it?

Cleaning Woman Very much.

Art It's just an old shirt.

Cleaning Woman It looks so well on you.

Art Why, thank you.

Cleaning Woman Not at all. (*Pause. Exits.*)

Art Form Form Form. Form and the use of tools.
Precision, restraint, control. (**Ed** *enters.*) Substance.
Meaning. The meaning of a thing. What it *means*. The *why*
of it. Walking. Beckoning. Biting . . . being bitten . . . The
acts of biting and of being bitten. Hopping and hoping.
(perhaps) Strangling and being strangled. And the acts of
perceiving those acts . . . The contract between oppressed
and oppressor. And who is who . . . and *why*.

Ed What are you talking about?

Art Just speaking in general.

Ed I'm unhappy here.

Art Why is that?

Ed (*pause*) We write the same thing all the time.

Art You think that I don't know that?

Ed I know you know that.

Art I know you do.

Ed And why do we do it?

Art And why do we do it?

Ed Why do you do it?

Art Why do I do it?

Ed Yes.

Art You'd be happier if we wrote something else? Is it the
squirrels you object to? To what is it that you object?
How can I make you happy?

Ed You're very overbearing.

Art Mmm.

Ed And I don't like it.

Art Well who would?

Ed I feel . . .

Art Yes?

Ed I feel . . .

Art Is it the squirrels that you object to? If that is it, please tell me. If that's what you object to we can move along to something else. Do you think that I'm fixated? Is that what you think? Do you think that? I am not tied to any one specific animal. Can you truly feel that I'm that limited? When you've been in the business as long as I you will not feel that way. There's more to life than a facility with modifiers. There's more to life than a flash in the pan. Some Johnnie-Come-Lately . . . and I try to make him happy . . . comes in here and I nurture him beneath my wing, give him the benefit of my experience, my expertise, my . . . uh . . .

Ed Exuberance.

Art And there you are, that's just my point. Exuberance indeed! When have you known me to be exuberant? Certainly the word begins with 'ex' but what of it, eh? What of it? Form form form. And you tell me you're unhappy here. Why? Can you tell me why? I'm not unhappy here.

Ed I'm sick of the squirrels.

Art You're sick of squirrels.

Ed Yes, I am.

Art Then we'll just write something else then, if it makes you so happy. There's more than one fish in the sea.

Ed I don't quite see how that applies.

Art You wouldn't.

Ed I don't.

Art Then just keep your mouth shut and shut up.

Pause. **Arthur** *fishes in wastebasket behind* **Edmond**'s *back – he* *takes out and reads the sheets the* **Cleaning Woman** *has discarded previously, and dictates the following.*

Take this down:
The moon. The moonlight.
The moonlight shone on the ocean right in
front of their tent. (eh?)
They had just crossed the desert. A desert
crossing lay behind them.
An ocean crossing lay in front of them as
they would have to cross the ocean.
They lay in the space between the two,
their limbs weary with fatigue, and, by
and by, they fell right off to sleep.

Now type that up, you sonofabitch, and get out of here.
I'll see you tomorrow in the morning. (*He exits*).

Interlude Three

At rise: *The* **Cleaning Woman** *and* **Edmond** *are creating. It is late at night.*

Cleaning Woman I almost saw a dog today that looked like a small horse.

Ed (*pause*) We've stopped working on the squirrels.

Cleaning Woman Yeah?

Ed We're writing about geese.

Cleaning Woman Ahhhhhh. A change is as good as a rest.

Ed Yes. Well, it seems to me that forward motion is an indication of progress. (*Pause.*) It seems to me that many times artistic achievement is difficult to measure. (*Pause.*) Artistic development is sometimes difficult to perceive. (*Pause.*) That sometimes that perception is not so crucial (*Pause.*) to the artist. (*Pause.*) That sometimes, rather than being productive . . . it has a potential for counterproductivity. Introspection. (*Pause.*) That a period of . . . work . . . untempered by harrassing elements of . . . introspective examination can be beneficial. (*Pause.*) Not the least potential accruing benefits of this being pedantic. (*Pause.*) That is, pedagogic. That is, that it is potentially not the least valuable aspect of this hiatic (non-introspective) period that it becomes, eventually, instructive. To the creator. (*Pause.*) I mean, lookit, he says 'Here! See how far I've come, and because I did the work and didn't worry those elements once only philosophic and ideal about which I wasted so much thought have become osmosed into my being as technique and are behind me.' (*Pause.*) This is how it seems to me. It seems to me that this is the way it is. That there is a strength (not to be scorned at) in technique. That the true employment of inspiration is in formal endeavors where the inspiration can take form. We *have* been working. It isn't as if we'd been idle. (*Pause.*)

We sat in our tent in the moonlight and
watched a flight of geese.
They flew in close formation.
Over the desert.
Making one drowsy.
And watched us fall asleep.

I wrote that.

Episode Four

At rise: **Arthur** *and* **Edmond** *are collaborating.*

Ed Geese.

Art Yes.

Ed Geese Geese Geese. Close in formation. Promoting order.

Art Making one drowsy.

Ed Up up up in the sky so blue.

Art (He's hot today.)

Ed Flying flying flying . . .

Art (he says everything three times)

Ed . . . high. How far to the bottom of the page?

Art Half an inch.

Ed Yes. Um . . .

Art They turn to each other . . . 'Dear, Dear,' he says. 'I almost saw a squirrel today that looked like a small dog . . .'

Ed Toss it out.

Art Yes?

Ed Toss it out, be free. Now pay attention. Geese.

Art Yes?

Ed Geese geese geese. Flying over park and lake. Over sand and water. Over sea and shore, young and old, lion and tiger. Searching searching searching. Searching to be free.

Long pause in which they look at each other with satisfaction.

Type it up and let's go home.

Epilogue

At rise: **Edmond** *and* **Arthur** *freeze at the end of Episode Four. The* **Cleaning Woman** *enters. She glances at her pad.*

Cleaning Woman
Squirrels. (Squirrels.)
Gatherers of nuts.
Harbingers of autumn.
Clucking and strangling.

Strangling and being strangled.
Rushing to your logical conclusion.
Searching to be free.

She assesses what she's written and throws it in the wastebasket.
She nods to the audience.

Blackout

American Buffalo

'Mine eyes have seen the glory of the coming of the Lord.
He is peeling down the alley in a black and yellow Ford.'

Folk Tune

The Characters:
Don Dubrow, *a man in his late forties, the owner of Don's Resale Shop*
Walter Cole, *called* **Teach**, *a friend and associate of Don*
Bob, *Don's gopher*

The Scene:
Don's Resale Shop. A junkshop.

The Time:
One Friday. Act One takes place in the morning. Act Two starts around 11.00 that night.

American Buffalo was first produced by the Goodman Theatre Stage Two, Chicago, Illinois, on 23 November 1975, with the following cast:

Bobby	William H. Macy
Teach	Bernard Erhard
Donny	J. J. Johnston

Directed by Gregory Mosher

In February 1976 it was showcased at St. Clement's, New York, with the following cast:

Bobby	J. T. Walsh
Teach	Mike Kellin
Donny	Michael Egan

Directed by Gregory Mosher

The New York Broadway production at the Ethel Barrymore Theatre opened on 16 February 1977, with the following cast:

Bobby	John Savage
Teach	Robert Duvall
Donny	Kenneth McMillan

Directed by Ulu Grosbard

The British première of *American Buffalo* opened at the National Theatre's Cottesloe auditorium on 28 June 1978, with the following cast:

Bobby	Michael Feast
Teach	Jack Shepherd
Donny	Dave King

Directed by Bill Bryden

American Buffalo was subsequently revived on Broadway with Al Pacino in the lead. On 24 July 1984 it opened at the Duke of York's Theatre, London, with the following cast:

Bobby	Bruce Macvittie
Teach	Al Pacino
Donny	J. J. Johnston

Directed by Arvin Brown

Note:
Some portions of the dialogue appear in parentheses, which serve to mark a slight change of outlook on the part of the speaker – perhaps a momentary change to a more introspective regard – D.M.

Act One

Don's Resale Shop. Morning. **Don** *and* **Bob** *are sitting.*

Don So?

Pause.

So what, Bob?

Pause.

Bob I'm sorry, Donny.

Pause.

Don All right.

Bob I'm sorry, Donny.

Pause.

Don Yeah.

Bob Maybe he's still in there.

Don If you think that, Bob, how come you're here?

Bob I came in.

Pause.

Don You don't come in, Bob. You don't come in until you do a thing.

Bob He didn't come out.

Don What do I care, Bob, if he came out or not? You're s'posed to watch the guy, you watch him. Am I wrong?

Bob I just went to the back.

Don Why?

Pause.

Why did you do that?

Bob 'Cause he wasn't coming out the front.

Don Well, Bob, I'm sorry, but this isn't good enough. If you want to do business . . . if we got a business deal, it isn't good enough. I want you to remember this.

Bob I do.

Don Yeah, *now* . . . but later, what?

Pause.

Just one thing, Bob. Action counts.

Pause.

Action talks and bullshit walks.

Bob I only went around to see he's coming out the back.

Don No, don't go fuck yourself around with these excuses.

Pause.

Bob I'm sorry.

Don Don't tell me that you're sorry. I'm not mad at you.

Bob You're not?

Don (*pause*) Let's clean up here.

Bob *starts to clean up the debris around the poker table.*

The only thing I'm trying to teach you something here.

Bob Okay.

Don Now lookit Fletcher.

Bob Fletch?

Don Now, Fletcher is a standup guy.

Bob Yeah.

Don I don't *give* a shit. He is a fellow stands for something –

Bob Yeah.

Don You take him and you put him down in some strange town with just a nickel in his pocket, and by nightfall he'll have that town by the balls. This is not talk, Bob, this is action.

Pause.

Bob He's a real good card player.

Don You're fucking A he is, Bob, and this is what I'm getting at. Skill. Skill and talent and the balls to arrive at your own *conclusions*.

The fucker won four hundred bucks last night.

Bob Yeah?

Don *Oh* yeah.

Bob And who was playing?

Don Me . . .

Bob Uh-huh . . .

Don And *Teach* . . .

Bob (How'd Teach do?)

Don (Not too good.)

Bob (No, huh?)

Don (No.) . . . and Earl was here . . .

Bob Uh-huh . . .

Don And Fletcher.

Bob *How'd* he do?

Don He won four hundred bucks.

Bob And who else won?

Don Ruthie, she won.

Bob She won, huh?

Don Yeah.

Bob She does okay.

Don *Oh* yeah . . .

Bob She's an okay card player.

Don Yes, she is.

Bob I like her.

Don Fuck, I like her, too. (There's nothing wrong in that.)

Bob (No.)

Don I mean, she treats you right.

Bob Uh-huh. How'd she do?

Don She did okay.

Pause.

Bob You win?

Don I did all right.

Bob Yeah?

Don Yeah. I did okay. Not like *Fletch* . . .

Bob No, huh?

Don I mean, Fletcher, he plays *cards*.

Bob He's real sharp.

Don You're goddamn right he is.

Bob I know it.

Don Was he born that way?

Bob Huh?

Don I'm saying was he born that way or do you think he had to learn it?

Bob Learn it.

Don Goddamn right he did, and don't forget it.

Everything, Bobby: it's going to happen to you, it's *not* going to happen to you, the important thing is can you deal with it, and can you *learn* from it.

Pause.

And this is why I'm telling you to stand up. It's no different with you than with anyone else. Everything that I or Fletcher know we picked up on the street. That's all business is . . . common sense, experience, and talent.

Bob Like when he jewed Ruthie out that pig iron.

Don What pig iron?

Bob That he got off her that time.

Don When was this?

Bob On the back of her truck.

Don That wasn't, I don't think, her pig iron.

Bob No?

Don That was *his* pig iron, Bob.

Bob Yeah?

Don Yeah. He bought it off her.

Pause.

Bob Well, she was real mad at him.

Don She was.

Bob Yup.

Don She was mad at him?

Bob Yeah. That he stole her pig iron.

Don He didn't steal it, Bob.

Bob No?

Don No.

Bob She was *mad* at him . . .

Don Well, that very well may be, Bob, but the fact remains that it was *business*. That's what business is.

Bob What?

Don People taking care of themselves. Huh?

Bob No.

Don 'Cause there's business and there's friendship, Bobby . . . there are many things, and when you walk around you *hear* a lot of things, and what you got to do is keep clear who your friends are, and who treated you like what. Or else the rest is garbage, Bob, because I want to tell you something.

Bob Okay.

Don Things are not always what they seem to be.

Bob I know.

Pause.

Don There's lotsa people on this street, Bob, they want this and they want that. Do anything to get it. You don't have *friends* this life . . . You want some breakfast?

Bob I'm not hungry.

Pause.

Don *Never* skip breakfast, Bob.

Bob Why?

Don Breakfast . . . is the most important meal of the day.

Bob I'm not hungry.

Don It makes no earthly difference in the world. You

know how much nutritive benefits they got in coffee? Zero. Not one thing. The stuff eats *you* up. You can't live on coffee, Bobby. (And I've told you this before.) You cannot live on cigarettes. You may feel *good*, you may feel *fine*, but something's getting overworked, and you are going to pay for it.

Now: What do you see me eat when I come in here every day?

Bob Coffee.

Don Come on, Bob, don't fuck with me. I *drink* a little coffee . . . but what do I eat?

Bob Yogurt.

Don Why?

Bob Because it's good for you.

Don You're goddamn right. And it wouldn't kill you to take a vitamin.

Bob They're too expensive.

Don Don't worry about it. You should just take 'em.

Bob I can't afford 'em.

Don Don't worry about it.

Bob You'll buy some for me?

Don Do you need 'em?

Bob *Yeah.*

Don Well, then, I'll get you some. What do you *think*?

Bob Thanks, Donny.

Don It's for your own good. Don't thank *me* . . .

Bob Okay.

Don I just can't use you in here like a zombie.

Bob I just went around the back.

Don I don't care. Do you see? Do you see what I'm getting at?

Pause.

Bob Yeah.

Pause.

Don Well, we'll see.

Bob I'm sorry, Donny.

Don Well, we'll see.

Teach (*appears in the doorway and enters the store*) Good morning.

Bob Morning, Teach.

Teach (*walks around the store a bit in silence*) Fuckin' Ruthie, fuckin' Ruthie, fuckin' Ruthie, fuckin' Ruthie, fuckin' Ruthie.

Don What?

Teach Fuckin' Ruthie . . .

Don . . . yeah?

Teach I come into the Riverside to get a cup of *coffee*, right? I sit down at the table Grace and Ruthie.

Don Yeah.

Teach I'm gonna order just a cup of coffee.

Don Right.

Teach So Grace and Ruthie's having breakfast, and they're done. *Plates . . . crusts* of stuff all over . . . So we'll shoot the shit.

Don Yeah.

Teach Talk about the *game* . . .

Don . . . yeah.

Teach . . . so on. Down I sit. 'Hi, hi.' I take a piece of toast off Grace's plate . . .

Don . . . uh-huh . . .

Teach . . . and she goes 'Help yourself.'

Help myself.

I should help myself to half a piece of toast it's four slices for a quarter. I should have a nickel everytime we're over at the game, I pop for coffee . . . cigarettes . . . a *sweet roll*, never say word.

'Bobby, see who wants what.' Huh? A fucking *roast-beef* sandwich. (*To* **Bob**.) Am I right? (*To* **Don**.) Ahh, shit. We're sitting down, how many times do I pick up the check? But (No!) because I never go and make a *big thing* out of it – it's no big thing – and flaunt like 'This one's on me' like some bust-out asshole, but I naturally assume that I'm with friends, and don't forget who's who when someone gets *behind* a half a yard or needs some help with (huh?) some fucking rent, or drops enormous piles of money at the track, or someone's *sick* or something . . .

Don (*to* **Bob**) This is what I'm talking about.

Teach Only (and I tell you this, Don). Only, and I'm not, I don't think, casting anything on anyone: from the mouth of a Southern bulldyke asshole ingrate of a vicious nowhere cunt can this trash come. (*To* **Bob**.) And I take nothing back, and I know you're close with them.

Bob With Grace and Ruthie?

Teach Yes.

Bob (I like 'em.)

Teach I have always treated everybody more than fair, and never gone around complaining. Is this true, Don?

Don Yup.

Teach Someone is *against* me, that's their problem . . . I can look out for myself, and I don't got to fuck around behind somebody's back, I don't like the way they're treating me. (Or pray some brick safe falls and hits them on the head, they're walking down the street.)

But to have that shithead turn, in one breath, every fucking sweet roll that I ever ate with them into *ground glass* (I'm wondering were they eating it and thinking 'This guy's an idiot to blow a fucking *quarter* on his friends' . . .)

. . . this hurts me, Don.

This hurts me in a way I don't know what the fuck to do.

Pause.

Don You're probably just upset.

Teach You're fuckin' A I'm upset. I am *very* upset, Don.

Don They got their problems, too, Teach.

Teach *I* would like to have their problems.

Don All I'm saying, nothing *personal* . . . they were probably, uh, *talking* about something.

Teach Then let them talk about it, then. No, I am sorry, Don, I cannot brush this off. They treat me like an asshole, they are an asshole.

Pause.

The only way to teach these people is to kill them.

Pause.

Don You want some coffee?

Teach I'm not hungry.

Don Come on, I'm sending Bobby to the Riverside.

Teach (Fuckin' joint . . .)

Don Yeah.

Teach (They harbor *assholes* in there . . .)

Don Yeah. Come on, Teach, what do you want? Bob?

Bob Yeah?

Don (*to* **Teach**) Come on, he's going anyway. (*To* **Bob**, *handing him a bill*.) Get me a Boston, and go for the yogurt.

Bob What kind?

Don You know, plain, and, if they don't got it, uh, something else. And get something for yourself.

Bob What?

Don Whatever you want. But get something to eat, and whatever you want to drink, and get Teacher a coffee.

Bob Boston, Teach?

Teach No.

Bob What?

Teach Black.

Bob Right.

Don And something for yourself to eat. (*To* **Teach**.) He doesn't want to eat.

Teach (*to* **Bob**) You got to eat (And this is what I'm saying at The Riverside.)

Pause.

Bob (Black coffee.)

Don And get something for yourself to eat. (*To* **Teach**.) What do you want to eat? An English muffin? (*To* **Bob**.) Get Teach an English muffin.

Teach I don't want an English muffin.

Don Get him an English muffin, and make sure they give you jelly.

Teach I don't want an English muffin.

Don What do you want?

Teach I don't want anything.

Bob Come on, Teach, eat something.

Pause.

Don You'll feel better you eat something, Teach.

Pause.

Teach (*to* **Bob**) Tell 'em to give you an order of bacon, real dry, real crisp.

Bob Okay.

Teach And tell the broad if it's for me she'll give you more.

Bob Okay.

Don Anything else you want?

Teach No.

Don A cantaloupe?

Teach I never eat cantaloupe.

Don No?

Teach It gives me the runs.

Don Yeah?

Teach And tell him he shouldn't say anything to Ruthie.

Don He wouldn't.

Teach No? No, you're right. I'm sorry, Bob.

Bob It's okay.

Teach I'm upset.

Bob It's okay, Teach.

Pause.

Teach Thank you.

Bob You're welcome.

Bob *starts to exit.*

Don And the plain if they got it.

Bob I will. (*Exits.*)

Don He wouldn't say anything.

Teach What the fuck do *I* care . . .

Pause.

Cunt.

Pause.

There is not one loyal bone in that bitch's body.

Don How'd you finally do last night?

Teach This has nothing to do with that.

Don No, I know. I'm just saying . . . for *talk* . . .

Teach Last night? You were here, Don.

Pause.

How'd *you* do?

Don Not well.

Teach Mmm.

Don The only one won any money, Fletch and Ruthie.

Teach (*pause*) Cunt had to win two hundred dollars.

Don She's a good card player.

Teach She is *not* a good card player, Don. She is a mooch and she is a locksmith and she plays like a woman.

Pause.

Fletcher's a card player, I'll give him that. But *Ruthie* . . . I mean, *you* see how she fucking plays . . .

Don Yeah.

Teach And always with that cunt on her shoulder.

Don Grace?

Teach Yes.

Don Grace is her partner.

Teach Then let her *be* her partner, then. (You see what I'm talking about?) Everyone, they're sitting at the table and then Grace is going to walk around . . . fetch an *ashtray* . . . go for *coffee* . . . *this* . . . and everybody's all they aren't going to hide their cards, and they're going to make a show how they don't hunch over, and like that. I don't give a shit. I say the broad's her fucking partner, and she walks in back of me I'm going to hide my hand.

Don Yeah.

Teach And I say anybody doesn't's out of their mind.

Pause.

We're talking about money for Chrissake, huh? We're talking about cards. Friendship is friendship, and a wonderful thing, and I am all for it. I have never said different, and you know me on this point.

Okay.

But let's just keep it *separate* huh, let's just keep the two apart, and maybe we can deal with each other like some human beings.

Pause.

This is all I'm saying, Don. I know you got a soft spot in your heart for Ruthie . . .

Don . . . yeah?

Teach I know you like the broad and Grace and, Bob, I know he likes 'em too.

Don (He likes 'em.)

Teach And I like 'em too. (I know, I know.) I'm not

averse to this. I'm not averse to sitting down. (I know we *will* sit down.) These things happen, I'm not saying that they don't . . . and yeah, yeah, yeah, I know I lost a bundle at the game and blah blah blah.

Pause.

But all I ever ask (and I would say this to her face) is only she remembers who is who and not to go around with *her* or Gracie either with this attitude. 'The Past is Past, and this is Now, and so Fuck You.'

You see?

Don Yes.

Long pause.

Teach So what's new?

Don Nothing.

Teach Same old shit, huh?

Don Yup.

Teach You seen my hat?

Don No. Did you leave it here?

Teach Yeah.

Pause.

Don You ask them over at The Riv?

Teach I left it here.

Pause.

Don Well, you left it here, it's here.

Teach You seen it?

Don No.

Pause.

Teach Fletch been in?

Don No.

Teach Prolly drop in one or so, huh?

Don Yeah, You know. You never know with Fletcher.

Teach No.

Don He might drop in the *morning* . . .

Teach Yeah.

Don And then he might, he's gone for ten or fifteen days you never know he's gone.

Teach Yeah.

Don Why?

Teach I want to talk to him.

Don (*pause*) Ruth would know.

Teach You sure you didn't seen my hat?

Don I didn't see it. No.

Pause.

Ruthie might know.

Teach (Vicious dyke.)

Don Look in the john.

Teach It isn't in the john. I wouldn't leave it there.

Don Do you got something up with Fletch?

Teach No. Just I have to talk to him.

Don He'll probably show up.

Teach Oh yeah . . . (*Pause. Indicating objects on the counter.*) What're *these*?

Don Those?

Teach Yeah.

Don They're from 1933.

Teach From the thing?

Don Yeah.

Pause.

Teach Nice.

Don They had a whole market in 'em. Just like anything. They license out the shit and everybody makes it.

Teach Yeah? (I knew that.)

Don Just like now. They had *combs*, and *brushes* . . . you know, brushes with the thing on 'em . . .

Teach Yeah. I know. They had . . . uh . . . what? Clothing too, huh?

Don I think. Sure. Everything. And there're guys they just collect the stuff.

Teach They got that much of it around?

Don *Shit* yes. (It's not that long ago.) The thing, it ran two years, and they had (*I* don't know) all kinds of people every year they're buying everything that they can lay their hands on that they're going to take it back to Buffalo to give it, you know, to their aunt, and it mounts up.

Teach What does it go for?

Don The compact?

Teach Yeah.

Don Aah . . . (*You* want it?)

Teach No.

Don Oh. I'm just asking. I mean, *you* want it . . .

Teach No. I mean somebody walks *in* here . . .

Don Oh. Somebody walks *in* here . . . (This shit's fashionable . . .)

Teach (I don't doubt it.)

Don . . . and they're gonna have to go like fifteen bucks.

Teach You're fulla shit.

Don My word of honor.

Teach No shit.

Don Everything like that.

Teach (A bunch of fucking thieves.)

Don Yeah. Everything.

Teach (*snorts*) What a bunch of crap, huh?

Don *Oh* yeah.

Teach Every goddamn thing.

Don Yes.

Teach If I kept the stuff that I threw out . . .

Don . . . yes.

Teach I would be a wealthy man today. I would be cruising on some European yacht.

Don Uh-huh.

Teach (Shit my father used to keep in his *desk* drawer.)

Don (My father, too.)

Teach (The *basement* . . .)

Don (Uh-huh.)

Teach (Fuckin' toys in the back*yard*, for Chrissake . . .)

Don (Don't even talk about it.)

Teach It's . . . I don't know.

Pause.

You want to play some gin?

Don Maybe later.

Teach Okay.

Pause.

I dunno.

Pause.

Fucking *day* . . .

Pause.

Fucking *weather* . . .

Pause.

Don You think it's going to rain?

Teach Yeah, I do. Later.

Don Yeah?

Teach Well, *look* at it.

Bob *appears, carrying a paper bag with coffee and foodstuffs in it.*

Bobby, Bobby, Bobby, Bobby, Bobby.

Bob Ruthie isn't mad at you.

Teach She isn't?

Bob No.

Teach How do you know?

Bob I found out.

Teach How?

Bob I talked to her.

Teach You talked to her.

Bob Yes.

Teach I asked you you weren't going to.

Bob Well, she asked me.

Teach What?

Bob That were you over here.

Teach What did you tell her?

Bob You were here.

Teach Oh. (*He looks at* **Don**.)

Don What did you say to her, Bob?

Bob Just Teach was here.

Don And is she coming over here?

Bob I don't think so. (They had the plain.)

Don (*to* **Teach**) So? (This is all right.)

(*To* **Bob**.) All right, Bob.

He looks at **Teach**.

Teach That's all right, Bob. (*To self.*) (Everything's all right to someone . . .)

Don *takes bag and distributes contents to appropriate recipients.*

(*To* **Don**.) You shouldn't eat that shit.

Don Why?

Teach It's just I have a feeling about health foods.

Don It's not health foods, Teach. It's only yogurt.

Teach That's not health foods?

Don No. They've had it forever.

Teach Yogurt?

Don Yeah. They used to joke about it on 'My Little Margie.' (*To* **Bob**.) (Way before your time.)

Teach Yeah?

Don Yeah.

Teach What the fuck. A little bit can't hurt you.

Don It's *good* for you.

Teach Okay, okay. Each one of his own opinion. (*Pause. To* **Bob**.) Was Fletcher over there?

Bob No.

Don Where's my coffee?

Bob It's not there?

Don No.

Pause.

Bob I told 'em specially to put it in.

Don Where *is* it?

Bob They forgot it.

Pause.

I'll go back and get it.

Don Would you mind?

Bob No.

Pause.

Don You gonna get it?

Bob Yeah.

Pause.

Don What, Bob?

Bob Can I talk to you?

Pause. **Don** *goes to* **Bob**.

Don What is it?

Bob I saw him.

Don Who?

Bob The guy.

Don You saw the guy?

Bob Yes.

Don That I'm talking about?

Bob Yes.

Don Just now?

Bob Yeah. He's going somewhere.

Don He is.

Bob Yeah. He's puttin' a suitcase in the car.

Don The guy, or both of 'em?

Bob Just him.

Don He got in the car he drove off??

Bob He's coming down the stairs . . .

Don Yeah.

Bob And he's got the suitcase . . .

Don *nods.*

He gets in the car . . .

Don Uh-huh . . .

Bob He drives away.

Don So where is she?

Bob He's goin' to pick her up.

Don What was he wearing?

Bob Stuff. Traveling clothes.

Don Okay.

Pause.

Now you're talking. You see what I mean?

Bob Ycah.

Don All right.

Bob And he had a coat, too.

Don Now you're talking.

Bob Like a raincoat.

Don Yeah.

Pause.

Good.

Pause.

Bob Yeah, he's gone.

Don Bob, go get me that coffee, do you mind?

Bob No.

Don What did you get yourself to eat?

Bob I didn't get anything.

Don Well, get me my coffee, and get yourself something to eat, okay?

Bob Okay. (Good.) (*Exits.*)

Pause.

Don How's your bacon?

Teach Aaaahh, they always fuck it up.

Don Yeah.

Teach This time they fucked it up too burnt.

Don Mmmm.

Teach You got to be breathing on their neck.

Don Mmmm.

Teach Like a lot of things.

Don Uh-huh.

Teach *Any* business . . .

Don Yeah.

Teach You want it run right, *be* there.

Don Yeah.

Teach Just like you.

Don What?

Teach Like the shop.

Don Well, no one's going to run it, I'm not here.

Pause.

Teach No.

Pause.

You have to be here.

Don Yeah.

Teach It's a one-man show.

Don Uh-huh.

Pause.

Teach So what is this thing with the kid?

Pause.

I mean, is it anything, uh . . .

Don It's nothing . . . *you* know . . .

Teach Yeah.

Pause.

It's *what* . . . ?

Don You know, it's just some *guy* we spotted.

Teach Yeah. Some *guy*.

Don Yeah.

Teach (Some guy . . .)

Don Yeah.

Pause.

What time is it?

Teach Noon.

Don (Noon.) (Fuck.)

Teach What?

Pause.

Don You parked outside?

Teach Yeah.

Don Are you okay on the meter?

Teach Yeah. The broad came by already.

Pause.

Don Good.

Pause.

Teach Oh, yeah, she came by.

Don Good.

Teach You want to tell me what this thing is?

Don (*pause*) The thing?

Teach Yeah.

Pause.

What is it?

Don Nothing.

Teach No? What is it, jewelry?

Don No. It's nothing.

Teach Oh.

Don You know?

Teach Yeah.

Pause.

Yeah. No. I don't know.

Pause.

Who am I, a *policeman* . . . I'm making conversation, huh?

Don Yeah.

Teach Huh?

Pause.

'Cause you know I'm just asking for talk.

Don Yeah. I know. Yeah, okay.

Teach And I can live without this.

Don (*reaches for phone*) Yeah, I know. Hold on, I'll tell you.

Teach Tell me if you *want* to, Don.

Don I want to, Teach.

Teach Yeah?

Don Yeah.

Pause.

Teach Well, I'd fucking hope so. Am I wrong?

Don No. No. You're right.

Teach I *hope* so.

Don No, hold on; I gotta make this call.

Teach Well, all right. So what is it, jewelry?

Don No.

Teach What?

Don Coins.

Teach (Coins).

Don Yeah. Hold on. I gotta make this call.

Don *hunts for a card, dials telephone.*

(*Into phone.*) Hello? This is Donny Dubrow. We were talking the other day. Lookit, sir, if I could get ahold of some of that stuff you were interested in, would you be interested in some of it.

Pause.

Those *things* . . . *Old*, yeah.

Pause.

Various pieces of various types.

Pause.

Tonight. Sometime late. Are they *what* . . . !!?? Yes, but I don't see what kind of a question is that (at the prices we're talking about . . .)

Pause.

No, hey, no, I understand *you* . . .

Pause.

Sometime late.

Pause.

One hundred percent.

Pause.

I feel the same. All right. Good-bye. (*Hangs up.*) Fucking asshole.

Teach Guys like that, I like to fuck their wives.

Don I don't blame you.

Teach Fucking *jerk* . . .

Don (I swear to God . . .)

Teach That guy's a collector?

Don Who?

Teach The phone guy.

Don Yeah.

Teach And the other guy?

Don We spotted?

Teach Yeah.

Don Him, too.

Teach So you hit him for his coins.

Don Yeah.

Teach – And you got a buyer in the phone guy.

Don (Asshole.)

Teach The thing is you're not sitting with the shit.

Don No.

Teach The guy's an asshole or he's not, what do you care? It's business.

Pause.

Don You're right.

Teach The guy with the suitcase, he's the mark.

Don Yeah.

Teach How'd you find him?

Don In here.

Teach Came in here, huh?

Don Yeah.

Teach (No shit.)

Pause.

Don He comes in here one day, like a week ago.

Teach For what?

Don Just browsing. So he's looking in the case, he comes up and with this *buffalo-head* nickel . . .

Teach Yeah . . .

Don From nine*teen*-something. (I don't know. I didn't even know it's there . . .)

Teach Uh-huh . . .

Don . . . and he goes, 'How much would that be?'

Teach Uh-huh . . .

Don So I'm about to go, 'Two bits,' jerk that I am, but something tells me to shut up, so I go, 'You tell me.'

Teach Always good business.

Don *Oh* yeah.

Teach How wrong can you go?

Don That's what I mean, so then he thinks a minute, and he tells me he'll just *shop* a bit.

Teach Uh-huh . . . (*Stares out of window.*)

Don And so he's *shopping* . . . What?

Teach Some cops.

Don Where?

Teach At the corner.

Don What are they doing?

Teach Cruising.

Pause.

Don They turn the corner?

Teach (*waits*) Yeah.

Pause.

Don . . . And so he's shopping. And he's picking up a beat-up *mirror* . . . and old *kid's* toy . . . a *shaving* mug . . .

Teach . . . right . . .

Don Maybe five, six things, comes to eight bucks I get 'em and put 'em in a box and then he tells me he'll go fifty dollars for the nickel.

Teach No.

Don Yeah. So I tell him (get this), 'Not a chance.'

Teach (Took balls.)

Don (Well, what-the-fuck . . .)

Teach (No, I mean it.)

Don (I took a chance.)

Teach (You're goddamn right.)

Pause.

Don (*shrugs*) So I say, 'Not a chance,' he tells me eighty is his highest offer.

Teach (I knew it.)

Don Wait. So I go, 'Ninety-five.'

Teach Uh-huh.

Don We settle down on ninety, *takes* the nickel, leaves the box of shit.

Teach He pay for it?

Don The box of shit?

Teach Yeah.

Don No.

Pause.

Teach And so what was the nickel?

Don *I* don't know . . . some rarity.

Teach Ninety dollars for a nickel.

Don Are you kidding, Teach? I bet it's worth *five times* that.

Teach Yeah, huh?

Don Are you kidding me, the guy is going to come in here, he plunks down ninety bucks like nothing. *Shit* yeah.

Pause.

Teach Well, what the fuck, it didn't cost you anything.

Don That's not the point. The next day back he comes and he goes through the whole bit again. He looks at *this*, he looks at *that*, it's a nice day . . .

Teach Yeah . . .

Don And he tells me he's the guy was in here yesterday and bought the buffalo off me and do I maybe have some other articles of interest.

Teach Yeah.

Don And so I tell him, 'Not offhand.' He says that could I get in touch with him, I get some in, so I say 'sure,' he leaves his card, I'm s'posed to call him anything crops up.

Teach Uh-huh.

Don He comes in here like I'm his fucking doorman.

Teach Mmmm.

Don He takes me off my coin and will I call him if I find another one.

Teach Yeah.

Don Doing me this favor by just coming in my shop.

Teach Yeah.

Pause.

Some people never change.

Don Like he has done me this big favor by just coming in my shop.

Teach Uh-huh. (You're going to get him now.)

Don (You know I am.) So Bob, we kept a lookout on his place, and that's the shot.

Teach And who's the chick?

Don What chick?

Teach You're asking Bob about

Don Oh yeah. The guy, he's married. I mean (*I* don't know.) We *think* he's married. They got two names on the bell. . . . Anyway, he's living with this chick, *you* know . . .

Teach What the hell.

Don . . . and you should see this chick.

Teach Yeah, huh?

Don She is a knockout. I mean, she is *real* nice-lookin', Teach.

Teach (Fuck *him* . . .)

Don The other day, last Friday like a week ago, Bob runs in, lugs me out to look at 'em, they're going out on bicycles. The ass on this broad, un-be-fucking-lievable in these bicycling shorts sticking up in the air with these short handlebars.

Teach (Fuckin' *fruits* . . .)

Pause.

Don So that's it. We keep an eye on 'em. They both work . . . (Yesterday he rode his bicycle to work.)

Teach He didn't.

Don Yeah.

Teach (*snorts*) (With the three-piece suit, huh?)

Don I didn't see 'em. Bobby saw 'em.

Pause.

And that's the shot. Earl gets me in touch the phone guy, he's this coin collector, and that's it.

Teach It fell in your lap.

Don Yeah.

Teach You're going in tonight.

Don It looks that way.

Teach And who's 'going in?'

Pause.

Don Bobby.

Pause.

Teach He's a great kid, Don. You know how I feel about the kid.

Pause.

I *like* him.

Don He's doing good.

Teach I can see that.

Pause.

But I gotta say something here.

Don What?

Teach Only this – and I don't think I'm *getting* at anything –

Don What?

Teach (*pause*) Don't send the kid in.

Don I shouldn't send Bobby in?

Teach No. (Now, just wait a second.) Let's siddown on this. What are we saying here? Loyalty.

Pause.

You know how I am on this. This is great. This is admirable.

Don What?

Teach This loyalty. This is swell. It turns my heart the things that you do for the kid.

Don What do I do for him, Walt?

Teach Things. Things, you know what I mean.

Don No. I don't do anything for him.

Teach In your mind you don't, but the things, I'm saying, that you actually go *do* for him. This is fantastic. All I mean, a guy can be too loyal, Don. Don't be dense on this. What are we saying here? Business.

I mean, the guy's got you're taking his high-speed blender and a Magnavox, you send the kid in. You're talking about a real *job* . . . they don't come in right away and know they been *had* . . .

You're talking maybe a safe, certainly a good lock or two, and you need a guy's looking for valuable shit, he's not going to mess with the stainless steel silverware, huh, or some digital clock.

Pause.

We both know what we're saying here. We both know we're talking about some job needs more than the kid's gonna skin-pop go in there with a *crowbar* . . .

Don I don't want you mentioning that.

Teach It slipped out.

Don You know how I feel on that.

Teach Yes. And I'm sorry, Don. I admire that. All that I'm saying, don't confuse business with pleasure.

Don But I don't want that talk, only, Teach.

Pause.

You understand?

Teach I more than understand, and I apologize.

Pause.

I'm sorry.

Don That's the only thing.

Teach All right. But I tell you. I'm glad I said it.

Don Why?

Teach 'Cause it's best for these things to be out in the open.

Don But I don't want it in the open.

Teach Which is why I apologized.

Pause.

Don You know the fucking kid's clean. He's trying hard, he's working hard, and you leave him alone.

Teach Oh yeah, he's trying *real* hard.

Don And he's no dummy, Teach.

Teach Far from it. All I'm saying, the job is beyond him. Where's the shame in this? This is not jacks, we get up to go home we give everything back. Huh? You want this fucked up?

Pause.

All that I'm saying, there's the least *chance* something might fuck up, you'd get the law down, you would take the shot, and you couldn't find the coins *whatever:* if you see the least chance, you cannot afford to take that chance! Don? *I* want to go in there and gut this motherfucker. Don? Where is the shame in this? You take care of him, *fine.* (Now this is loyalty.) But Bobby's got his own best interests, too. And you cannot afford (and simply as a *business* proposition) you cannot afford to take the chance.

(*Pause.* **Teach** *picks up a strange object.*) What is this?

Don That?

Teach Yes.

Don It's a thing that they stick in dead pigs keep their legs apart all the blood runs out.

Teach *nods. Pause.*

Teach Mmmm.

Pause.

Don I set it up with him.

Teach 'You set it up with him.' . . . You set it up and then you told him.

Long pause.

Don I gave Earl ten percent.

Teach Yeah? for what?

Don The connection.

Teach So ten off the top: forty-five, forty-five.

Pause.

Don And Bobby?

Teach A hundred. A hundred fifty . . . we hit big . . . *whatever.*

Don And *you* what?

Teach The *shot.* I go, I go *in* . . . I bring the stuff *back* (or wherever . . .)

Pause.

Don And what do I do?

Teach You mind the fort.

Pause.

Don Here?

Teach Well, yeah . . . this is the fort.

Pause.

Don (You know, this is real classical money we're talking about.)

Teach I know it. You think I'm going to fuck with Chump Change?

Pause.

So tell me.

Don Well, hold on a second. I mean, we're still talking.

Teach I'm sorry. I thought we were done talking.

Don No.

Teach Well, then, let's talk some more. You want to bargain? You want to mess with the points?

Don No. I just want to think for a second.

Teach Well, you think, but here's a helpful hint. Fifty percent of some money is better than ninety percent of some broken *toaster* that you're gonna have, you send the kid in. (Which is providing he don't trip the alarm in the *first* place . . .) Don? You don't even know what the *thing* is on this. Where he lives. They got alarms? What *kind* of alarms? What kind of *this* . . . ? And what if (God forbid) the *guy* walks in? Somebody's nervous, whacks him with a table lamp – you wanna get touchy – and you can take your ninety dollars from the nickel shove it up your ass – the good it did you – and you wanna know *why*? (And I'm not *saying* anything . . .) because you didn't take the time to go first-class.

Bob *re-enters with a bag.*

Hi, Bob.

Bob Hi, Teach.

Pause.

Don You get yourself something to eat?

Bob I got a piece of pie and a Pepsi.

Bob and **Don** *extract foodstuffs and eat.*

Don Did they charge you again for the coffee?

Bob For your coffee?

Don Yes.

Bob They charged me this time. I don't know if they charged me last time, Donny.

Don It's okay.

Pause.

Teach (*to* **Bob**) How is it out there?

Bob It's okay.

Teach Is it going to rain?

Bob Today?

Teach Yeah.

Bob I don't know.

Pause.

Teach Well, what do you think?

Bob It might.

Teach You think so, huh?

Don Teach . . .

Teach What? I'm not saying anything.

Bob What?

Teach I don't think I'm saying anything here.

Pause.

Bob It *might* rain.

Pause.

I think *later*.

Teach How's your pie?

Bob Real good.

Teach (*holds up the dead-pig leg-spreader*) You know what this is?

Pause.

Bob Yeah.

Teach What is it?

Bob I know what it is.

Teach What?

Bob I know.

Pause.

Teach Huh?

Bob What?

Teach Things are what they are.

Don Teach . . .

Teach What?

Don We'll do this later.

Bob I got to ask you something.

Teach Sure, that makes a difference.

Don We'll just do it later.

Teach Sure.

Bob Uh, Don?

Don What?

Pause.

Bob I got to talk to you.

Don Yeah? What?

Bob I'm wondering on the thing that maybe I could have a little bit up front.

Pause.

Don Do you *need* it?

Bob I don't *need* it . . .

Don How much?

Bob I was thinking that maybe you might let me have like fifty or something.

Pause.

To sort of *have* . . .

Teach You got any cuff links?

Don Look in the case. (*To* **Bob**) What do you need it for?

Bob Nothing.

Don Bob . . .

Bob You can trust me.

Don It's not a question of that. It's not a question I go around trusting you, Bob . . .

Bob What's the question?

Teach Procedure.

Don Hold on, Teach.

Bob I got him all spotted.

Pause.

Teach Who?

Bob Some guy.

Teach Yeah?

Bob Yeah.

Teach Where's he live?

Bob Around.

Teach Where? Near here?

Bob No.

Teach No?

Bob He lives like on Lake Shore Drive.

Teach He does.

Bob Yeah.

Teach (*pause*) What have you got, a job cased?

Bob I just went for coffee.

Teach But you didn't *get* the coffee.

Pause.

Now, did you?

Bob No.

Teach Why?

Don Hold on, Teach. Bob . . .

Bob What?

Don You know what?

Bob No.

Don I was thinking, you know, we might hold off on this thing.

Pause.

Bob You wanna hold off on it?

Don I was thinking that we might.

Bob Oh.

Don And, on the money, I'll give you . . . forty, you owe me twenty, and, for now, keep twenty for spotting the guy.

Pause.

Okay?

Bob Yeah.

Pause.

You don't want me to do the job?

Don That's what I *told* you. What am I telling you?

Bob I'm not going to do it.

Don Not *now*. We aren't going to do it now.

Bob We'll do it later on?

Don (*shrugs*) But I'm giving you twenty just for spotting the guy.

Bob I need fifty, Donny.

Don Well, I'm giving you forty.

Bob You said you were giving me twenty.

Don No, Bob, I did not. I said I was giving you forty, of *which* you were going to owe me twenty.

Pause.

And you go *keep* twenty.

Bob I got to give back twenty.

Don That's the deal.

Bob When?

Don Soon. When you got it.

Pause.

Bob If I don't *get* it soon?

Don Well, what do you call 'soon'?

Bob I don't know.

Don Could you get it in a . . . day, or a couple of days or so?

Bob Maybe. I don't *think* so. Could you let me have fifty?

Don And you'll give me back thirty?

Bob I could just give back the twenty.

Don That's not the deal.

Bob We could *make* it the deal.

Pause.

Donny? We could *make* it the deal. Huh?

Don Bob, lookit. Here it is: I give you fifty, next week you pay me back twenty-five.

Pause.

You get to keep twenty-five, you pay me back twenty-five.

Bob And what about the thing?

Don Forget about it.

Bob You tell me when you want me to do it.

Don I don't know *that* I want you to do it. At this point.

Pause.

You know what I mean?

Pause.

Bob No.

Don I mean, I'm *giving* you twenty-five, and I'm saying forget the thing.

Bob Forget it for me.

Don Yes.

Bob Oh.

Pause.

Okay. Okay.

Don You see what I'm talking about?

Bob Yes.

Don Like it never happened.

Bob I know.

Don So you see what I'm saying.

Bob Yes.

Pause.

I'm gonna go.

Pause.

I'll see you later. (*Pause. He looks at* **Don**.)

Don Oh. (*Reaches in pocket and hands bills to* **Bob**. *To* **Teach**.) You got two fives?

Teach No.

Don (*to* **Bob**) I got to give you . . . thirty, you owe me back thirty.

Bob You said you were giving me fifty.

Don I'm sorry, I'm sorry, Bob, you're absolutely right. (*He gives* **Bob** *remainder of money*.)

Pause.

Bob Thank you.

Pause.

I'll see you later, huh, Teach?

Teach I'll see you later, Bobby.

Bob I'll see you, Donny.

Don I'll see you later, Bob.

Bob I'll come back later.

Don Okay.

Bob *starts to exit.*

Teach See you.

Pause. **Bob** *is gone.*

You're only doing the right thing by him, Don.

Pause.

Believe me.

Pause.

It's best for everybody.

Pause.

What's done is done.

Pause.

So let's get started. On the thing. Tell me everything.

Don Like what?

Teach . . . the *guy* . . . where does he *live* . . .

Don Around the corner.

Teach Okay, and he's gone for the weekend.

Don We don't know.

Teach Of course we know. Bob saw him coming out the door. The kid's not going to lie to you.

Don Well, Bob just saw him coming *out* . . .

Teach He had a suitcase, Don, he wasn't going to the A&P . . . He's going for the weekend . . .

Pause.

Don, (Can you cooperate?) Can we get started? Do you want to tell me something about coins?

Pause.

Don What about 'em?

Teach A crash course. What to look for. What to take. What to *not* take (. . . this they can trace) (that isn't *worth* nothing . . .)

Pause.

What looks like what but it's more *valuable* . . . so on . . .

Don First off, I want that nickel back.

Teach Donny . . .

Don No, I know, it's only a fuckin' nickel . . . I mean big deal, huh? But what I'm saying is I only want it back.

Teach You're going to get it back. I'm going in there for his coins, what am I going to take 'em all except your nickel? Wake up. Don, let's plan this out. The *spirit* of the thing?

Pause.

Let's not be loose on this. People are *loose*, people pay the price . . .

Don You're right.

Teach (And I like you like a brother, Don.) So let's wake up on this.

Pause.

All right? A man, he walks in here, well-dressed . . . (With a briefcase?)

Don (No.)

Teach All right . . . comes into a junkshop looking for coins.

Pause.

He spots a valuable nickel hidden in a pile of shit. He farts around, he picks up this, he farts around, he picks up that.

Don (He wants the nickel.)

Teach No shit. He goes to check out, he goes ninety on the nick.

Don (He would of gone five times that.)

Teach (Look, don't kick yourself.) All right, we got a guy knows coins. Where does he keep his coin collection?

Don Hidden.

Teach The man hides his coin collection, we're probably looking the guy has a *study* . . . I mean, he's not the kind of guy to keep it in the *basement* . . .

Don No.

Teach So we're looking for a study.

Don (A den.)

Teach And we're looking, for, he hasn't got a safe . . .

Don Yeah . . . ?

Teach . . . he's probably going to keep 'em . . . where?

Pause.

Don I don't know. His desk drawer.

Teach (You open the middle, the rest of 'em pop out?)

Don (Yeah.)

Teach (Maybe.) Which brings up a point.

Don What?

Teach As we're moving the stuff tonight, we can go in like Gangbusters, huh? We don't care we wreck the joint up. So what else? We *take* it, or leave it?

Don . . . well . . .

Teach I'm not talking *cash*, all I mean, what other stuff do we take . . . for our *trouble* . . .

Pause.

Don I don't know.

Teach It's hard to make up rules about this stuff.

Don (You'll be in there under lots of pressure.)

Teach (Not so much.)

Don (Come on, a little, anyway.)

Teach (That's only natural.)

Don (Yeah.)

Teach (It would be unnatural I wasn't tense. A guy who isn't tense, I don't want him on my side.)

Don (No.)

Teach (You know *why*?)

Don (Yeah.)

Teach (Okay, then.) It's good to talk this stuff out.

Don Yeah.

Teach You *have* to talk it out. Bad feelings, misunderstandings happen on a job. You can't get away from 'em, you have to deal with 'em. You want to quiz me on some coins? You want to show some coins to me? *List* prices . . . the blue book . . . ?

Don You want to see the book?

Teach Sure.

Don (*hands large coin-book to* **Teach**) I just picked it up last week.

Teach Uh-hum.

Don All the values aren't *current* . . .

Teach Uh-huh . . .

Don *Silver* . . .

Teach (*looking at book*) Uh-huh . . .

Don What's *rarity* . . .

Teach Well, that's got to be fairly steady, huh?

Don I'm saying against what *isn't*.

Teach Oh.

Don But the book gives you a general idea.

Teach You've been looking at it?

Don Yeah.

Teach You got to have a feeling for your subject.

Don The book can give you that.

Teach This is what I'm *saying* to you. One thing. Makes all the difference in the world.

Don What?

Teach Knowing what the fuck you're talking about. And it's so rare, Don. So rare.

What do you think a 1929 S Lincoln-head penny with the wheat on the back is worth?

Don *starts to speak*.

Ah! Ah! Ah! Ah! Ah! We got to know what *condition* we're talking about.

Don (*pause*): Okay. What condition?

Teach Any of 'em. You tell me.

Don Well, pick one.

Teach Okay, I'm going to pick an easy one. Excellent condition 1929 S.

Don It's worth . . . *about* thirty-six dollars.

Teach No.

Don (More?)

Teach Well, guess.

Don Just tell me is it more or less.

Teach What do you think?

Don More.

Teach No.

Don Okay, it's worth, I gotta say . . . eighteen-sixty.

Teach No.

Don Then I give up.

Teach Twenty fucking cents.

Don You're fulla shit.

Teach My mother's grave.

Don Give me that fucking book. (*Business*.) Go beat that.

Teach This is what I'm saying, Don, you got to know what you're talking about.

Don You wanna take the book?

Teach Naaa, *fuck* the book. What am I going to do, leaf through the book for hours on end? The important thing is to have the *idea* . . .

Don Yeah.

Teach What was the other one?

Don What other one?

Teach He stole off you.

Don What do you mean what was it?

Teach The *date*, so on.

Don How the fuck do *I* know?

Teach (*pause*) When you looked it up.

Don How are you getting in the house?

Teach The house?

Don Yeah.

Teach Aah, you go in through a *window* they left open, something.

Don Yeah.

Teach There's always something.

Don Yeah, What else, if not the window.

Teach How the fuck do *I* know?

Pause.

If not the window, something else.

Don What?

Teach We'll see when we get there.

Don Okay, all I'm asking, what it *might* be.

Teach Hey, you didn't warn us we were going to have a *quiz* . . .

Don It's just a question.

Teach I know it.

Pause.

Don What is the answer?

Teach We're seeing when we get there.

Don Oh. You can't answer me, Teach?

Teach You have your job, I have my job, Don. I am not here to smother you in theory. Think about it.

Don I am thinking about it. I'd like you to answer my question.

Teach Don't push me, Don. Don't front off with me here. I am not other people.

Don And just what does that mean?

Teach Just that nobody's perfect.

Don They aren't.

Teach No.

Pause.

Don I'm going to have Fletch come with us.

Teach Fletch.

Don Yes.

Teach You're having him *come* with us.

Don Yes.

Teach Now you're kidding me.

Don No.

Teach No? Then why do you say this?

Don With Fletch.

Teach Yes.

Don I want some depth.

Teach You want depth on the team.

Don Yes, I do.

Teach So you bring in Fletch.

Don Yes.

Teach 'Cause I don't play your games with you.

Don We just might need him.

Teach We won't.

Don We might, Teach.

Teach We don't need him, Don. We do not need this guy.

Don *picks up phone.*

What? Are you calling him?

Don *nods.*

Don It's busy. (*Hangs up.*)

Teach He's probably talking on the phone.

Don Yeah. He probably is.

Teach We don't need this guy, Don. We don't need him. I see your point here, I do. So you're thinking I'm out there alone, and you're worried I'll rattle, so you ask me how I go in. I understand. I see this, I do. I could go in the second floor, climb up a drainpipe, I could *this* . . .

Don *dials phone again.*

He's talking, he's talking, for Chrissake, give him a minute, huh?

Don *hangs up phone.*

I am hurt, Don.

Don I'm sorry, Teach.

Teach I'm not hurt for me.

Don Who are you hurt for?

Teach Think about it.

Don We can use somebody watch our rear.

Teach You keep your numbers down, you don't *have* a rear. You know what has rears? Armies.

Don I'm just saying, something goes *wrong* . . .

Teach Wrong, wrong, you make your own right and wrong. Hey Biiig fucking deal. The shot is yours, no one's disputing that. We're talking business, let's *talk* business: you think it's good business call Fletch in? To help us.

Don Yes.

Teach Well then okay.

Pause.

Are you sure?

Don Yeah.

Teach All right, if you're *sure* . . .

Don I'm sure, Teach.

Teach Then, all right, then. That's all I worry about.

Pause.

And you're probably right, we could use three of us on the job.

Don Yeah.

Teach Somebody watch for the *cops* . . . work out a *signal* . . .

Don Yeah.

Teach Safety in numbers.

Don Yeah.

Teach Three-men jobs.

Don Yeah.

Teach You, me, Fletcher.

Don Yeah.

Teach A division of labor.

Pause.

(Security. Muscle. Intelligence.) Huh?

Don Yeah.

Teach This means, what, a traditional split. Am I right? We get ten off the top goes to Earl, and the rest, three-way split. Huh? That's what we got? Huh?

Don Yeah.

Teach Well, that's what's right.

Pause.

All right. Lay the shot out for me.

Don For tonight?

Teach Yes.

Don Okay.

Pause.

I stay here on the phone . . .

Teach . . . yeah . . .

Don . . . for Fletcher . . .

Teach Yeah.

Don We meet, ten-thirty, 'leven, back here.

Teach (Back here, the three . . .)

Don Yeah. And go in.

Pause.

Huh?

Teach Yeah. Where?

Don Around the corner.

Teach Yeah.

Pause.

Are you mad at me?

Don No.

Teach Do you want to play gin?

Don Naaa.

Teach Then I guess I'll go home, take a nap, and rest up. Come back here tonight and we'll take off this fucking fruit's coins.

Don Right.

Teach I feel like I'm trying to stay *up* to death . . .

Don You ain't been to sleep since the game?

Teach *Shit* no (then that dyke cocksucker . . .)

Don So go take a nap. You trying to kill yourself?

Teach You're right, and you do what you think is right, Don.

Don I got to, Teach.

Teach You got to trust your instincts, right or wrong.

Don I got to.

Teach I know it. I know you do.

Pause.

Anybody wants to get in touch with me, I'm over the hotel.

Don Okay.

Teach I'm not the *hotel*, I stepped out for coffee, I'll be back one minute.

Don Okay.

Teach And I'll see you around eleven.

Don *O'clock.*

Teach *Here.*

Don Right.

Teach And don't worry about anything.

Don I won't.

Teach I don't want to hear you're worrying about a goddamned thing.

Don You won't, Teach.

Teach You're sure you want Fletch coming with us?

Don Yes.

Teach All right, then, so long as you're sure.

Don I'm sure, Teach.

Teach Then I'm going to see you tonight.

Don Goddamn right you are.

Teach I am seeing you later.

Don I know.

Teach Good-bye.

Don Good-bye.

Teach I want to make one thing plain before I go, Don. I am not mad at you.

Don I know.

Teach All right, then.

Don You have a good nap.

Teach I will.

Teach *exits.*

Don Fuckin' *business* . . .

Lights dim to black.

Act Two

Don's Resale Shop. 11:15 that evening. The shop is darkened. **Don** *is alone. He is holding the telephone to his ear.*

Don Great. Great great great great great.

Pause.

(*Cocksucking fuckhead* . . .)

Pause.

This is greatness.

Don *hangs up phone.* **Bob** *appears in the door to the shop.*

What are you doing here?

Bob I *came* here.

Don For what?

Bob I got to talk to you.

Don Why?

Bob Business.

Don Yeah?

Bob I need some money.

Don What for?

Bob Nothing. I can pay for it.

Don For what?

Bob This guy. I found a coin.

Don A coin?

Bob A buffalo-head.

Don Nickel?

Bob Yeah. You want it?

Pause.

Don What are you doing here, Bob?

Bob I need money.

Don *picks up phone and dials. He lets it ring as he talks to* **Bob.**

You want it?

Don What?

Bob My buffalo.

Don Lemme look at it.

Pause.

I got to look at it to know do I want it.

Bob You don't know if you want it?

Don I probably *want* it . . . what I'm saying, if it's *worth* anything.

Bob It's a buffalo, it's worth something.

Don The question is but what. It's just like everything else, Bob. Like every other fucking thing. (*Pause. He hangs up phone.*) Were you at The Riv?

Bob Before.

Don Is Fletch over there?

Bob No.

Don Teach?

Bob No. Ruth and Gracie was there for a minute.

Don What the fuck does that mean?

Pause.

Bob Nothing.

Pause.

Only they were there.

Pause.

I didn't *mean* anything . . . my nickel . . . I can tell you what it is.

Pause.

I can tell you what it is.

Don What? What *date* it is? That don't mean shit.

Bob No?

Don Come *on*, Bobby? What's important in a coin . . .

Bob . . . yeah?

Don What *condition* it's in . . .

Bob (Great.)

Don . . . if you can (I don't know . . .) count the hair on the Indian, something. You got to look it up.

Bob In the book?

Don Yes.

Bob Okay. And then you know.

Don Well, no. What I'm saying, the book is like you use it like an *indicator* (I mean, right off with *silver* prices . . . so on . . .) (*He hangs up phone.*) Shit.

Bob What?

Don What do you want for the coin?

Bob What it's worth only.

Don Okay, we'll look it up.

Bob But you still don't know.

Don But you got an idea, Bob. You got an idea you can deviate from.

Pause.

Bob The other guy went ninety bucks.

Don He was a fuckin' sucker, Bob.

Pause.

Am I a sucker? (Bob, I'm busy here. You see?)

Bob Some coins are worth that.

Don Oddities, Bob. Freak oddities of nature. What are we talking about here? The silver? The silver's maybe three times face. You want fifteen cents for it?

Bob No.

Don So, okay. So what do you want for it?

Bob What it's worth.

Don Let me see it.

Bob Why?

Don To look in the goddamn . . . Forget it. Forget it. *Don't* let me see it.

Bob But the book don't *mean* shit.

Don The book gives us *ideas*, Bob. The book gives us a basis for *comparison*.

Look, we're human beings. We can *talk*, we can negotiate, we can *this* . . . you need money? What do you need?

Pause.

Bob I *came* here . . .

Pause.

Don What do you need, Bob?

Pause.

Bob How come you're in here so late?

Don We're gonna play cards.

Bob Who?

Don Teach and me and Fletcher.

Teach *enters the store.*

What time is it?

Teach Fuck is *he* doing here?

Don What fucking time is it?

Teach Where's Fletcher?

Pause.

Where's Fletcher?

Bob Hi, Teach.

Teach (*to* **Don**) What is he doing here?

Bob I came in.

Don Do you know what time it is?

Teach What? I'm late?

Don Damn right you're late.

Teach I'm fucked up since my watch broke.

Don Your watch broke?

Teach I just told you that.

Don When did your watch break?

Teach The fuck do *I* know?

Don Well, you look at it. You want to know your watch broke, all you got to do is look at it.

Pause.

Teach I don't have it.

Don Why not?

Teach I took it off when it broke. (What do you *want* here?)

Don You're going around without a watch.

Teach Yes. I am, Donny. What am I, you're my *keeper* all a sudden?

Don I'm paying you to do a thing, Teach, I expect to know where you are when.

Teach Donny. You aren't paying me to do a thing. We are doing something together. I know we are. My watch broke, that is my concern. The *thing* is your and my concern. And the concern of Fletcher. You want to find a reason we should jump all over each other all of a sudden like we work in a *bloodbank*, fine. But it's not good business.

Pause.

And so who knows what time it is offhand? Jerks on the radio? The phone broad?

Pause.

Now, I understand nerves.

Don There's no fuckin' nerves involved in this. Teach.

Teach No, huh?

Don No.

Teach Well, great. That's great, then. So what are we talking about? A little lateness? Some excusable fucking lateness? And a couple of guys they're understandably a bit excited?

Pause.

Don I don't like it.

Teach Then *don't* like it, then. Let's do this. Let's everybody get a writ. I got a case. You got a case. Bobby – I don't know what the fuck *he's* doing here . . .

Don Leave him alone.

Teach Now I'm picking on him.

Don Leave him alone.

Teach What's he doing here?

Don He came in.

Bob I found a nickel.

Teach Hey, that's fantastic.

Bob You want to see it?

Teach Yes, please let me see it.

Bob (*hands nickel, wrapped in cloth, to* **Teach**) I like 'em because of the art on it.

Teach Uh-huh.

Bob Because it *looks* like something.

Teach (*to* **Don**) Is this worth anything?

Bob We don't know yet.

Teach Oh.

Bob We're going to look it up.

Teach Oh, what? Tonight?

Bob I think so.

Don (*hangs up phone*) Fuck.

Teach So where is he?

Don How the fuck do I know?

Teach He said he'd be here?

Don Yes, he did, Teach.

Bob Fletcher?

Teach So where is he, then? And what's *he* doing here?

Don Leave him alone. He'll leave.

Teach He's going to leave, huh?

Don Yes.

Teach You're sure it isn't like the bowling league, Fletch doesn't show up, we just suit up Bobby, give him a shot, and *he* goes in?

Pause.

Aaah, fuck. I'm sorry. I spoke in anger. I'm sorry, I'm sorry. (Everybody can make mistakes around here but me.) I'm sorry, Bob, I'm very sorry.

Bob That's okay, Teach.

Teach All I meant to say, we'd give you a fuckin' suit, like in football . . .

Pause.

and you'd (You know, like, whatever . . .) and *you'd* go in. (*Pause. To* **Don**) So what do you want me to do? Dress up and lick him all over? I said I was sorry, what's going on here. Huh? In the *first* place. I come in, I'm *late* . . . *he's* here . . .

Pause.

Don Bobby, I'll see you tomorrow, okay? (*He picks phone up and dials.*)

Bob I need some money.

Teach (*digging in pockets*) What do you need?

Bob I want to sell the *buffalo* nickel.

Teach I'll buy it myself.

Bob We don't know what it's worth.

Teach What do you want for it?

Bob Fifty dollars.

Teach You're outta your fuckin' mind.

Pause.

Look. Here's a fin. Get lost. Okay?

Pause.

Bob It's worth more than that.

Teach How the fuck do you know that?

Bob I think it is.

Pause.

Teach Okay. You keep the fin like a loan. You *keep* the fuckin' nickel, and we'll call it a loan. Now go on. (*He hands nickel back to* **Bob**.)

Don (*hangs up phone*) Fuck.

Bob I need more.

Teach (*to* **Don**) Give the kid a couple of bucks.

Don What?

Teach Give him some money.

Don What for?

Teach The nickel.

Pause.

Bob We can look in the book tomorrow.

Don (*to* **Teach**) You bought the nickel?

Teach Don't worry about it. Give him some money. Get him out of here.

Don How much?

Teach What? *I* don't care . . .

Don (*to* **Bob**) How much . . . (*To* **Teach**) What the fuck am I giving him money for?

Teach Just give it to him.

Don What? Ten? (*Pause. Digs in pocket, hands bill to* **Bob**.)

How is that, Bob? (*Pause. Hands additional bill to* **Bob**.)
Okay?

Bob We'll look it up.

Don Okay. Huh? We'll see you tomorrow.

Bob And we'll look it up.

Don Yes.

Bob (*to* **Teach**) You should talk to Ruthie.

Teach Oh, I should, huh?

Bob Yes.

Teach Why?

Bob Because.

Pause.

Teach I'll see you tomorrow, Bobby.

Bob Good-bye, Teach.

Teach Good-bye.

Don Good-bye, Bob.

Bob Good-bye.

Pause. **Bob** *exits.*

Don Fuckin' *kid* . . .

Teach So where is Fletcher?

Don Don't worry. He'll be here.

Teach The question is but when. Maybe his watch broke.

Don Maybe it just did, Teach. Maybe his actual watch broke.

Teach And maybe mine didn't, you're saying? You
wanna bet? You wanna place a little fucking wager on it?
How much money you got in your pockets? I bet you all
the money in your pockets against all the money in my

pockets, I walk out that door right now, I come back with a broken watch.

Pause.

Don Calm down.

Teach I am calm. I'm just upset.

Don I know.

Teach So where is he when I'm here?

Don Don't worry about it.

Teach So who's going to worry about it then?

Don (Shit.)

Teach This should go to prove you something.

Don It doesn't prove anything. The guy's just late.

Teach Oh. And I wasn't?

Don You were late, too.

Teach You're fuckin' A I was, and I got bawled out for it.

Don He's late for a reason.

Teach I don't accept it.

Don That's your privilege.

Teach And what was Bob doing here?

Don He told you. He wanted to sell me the nickel.

Teach That's why he came here?

Don Yes.

Teach To sell you the buffalo?

Don Yes.

Teach Where did he get it?

Don I think from some guy.

Teach Who?

Pause.

Don I don't know.

Pause.

Teach Where's Fletcher?

Don I don't know. He'll show up. (*Picks up phone and dials.*)

Teach He'll show up.

Don Yes.

Teach He's not here now.

Don No.

Teach You scout the guy's house?

Don The guy? No.

Teach Well, let's do that, then. (He's not home. Hang up.)

Don (*hangs up phone*) You wanna scout his house.

Teach Yeah.

Don Why? Bob already saw him when he went off with the suitcase.

Teach Just to be sure, huh?

Don Yeah. Okay.

Teach You bet. Now we call him up.

Don We call the guy up.

Teach Yeah.

Pause.

Don Good idea. (*He picks up phone. Hunts guy's number. Dials. To himself*) We can do this.

Teach This is planning . . . This is preparation. If he answers . . .

Don *shhhhs* **Teach**.

I'm telling you what to do if he answers.

Don What?

Teach Hang up. (**Don** *starts to hang up phone*.) No. *Don't* hang up. Hang up now. Hang up *now*!

Don *hangs up phone*.

Now look: If he *answers* . . .

Don . . . yeah?

Teach *Don't* arouse his fucking suspicions.

Don All right.

Teach And the odds are he's not there, so when he answers just say you're calling for a wrong fucking *number*, something. Be simple.

Pause.

Give me the phone.

Don *hands* **Teach** *the phone*.

Gimme the card.

Don *hands* **Teach** *card*.

This is his number? 221-7834?

Don Yeah.

Teach (*snorts*) All right. I dial, I'm calling for somebody named June, and we go interchange on number.

Pause.

We're gonna say like, 'Is this 221-7834?'

Don . . . yeah?

Teach And they go, 'No.' (I mean '-7843.' It *is* -7834.) So we go, very simply, 'Is this 221-7843?' and they go 'No,' and right away the guy is home, we still haven't blown the shot.

Don Okay.

Teach *picks up the phone and dials.*

Teach (*into phone*) Hi. Yeah. I'm calling . . . uh . . . is June there?

Pause.

Well, is this 221-7843?

Pause.

It is? Well, look I must of got the number wrong. I'm sorry.

He hangs up phone.

(This is bizarre.) Read me that number.

Don 221-7834.

Teach Right. (*Dials phone. Listens.*) Nobody home. See, this is careful operation . . . (*Pause. Hangs up.*) You wanna try it?

Don No.

Teach I don't mind that you're careful, Don. This doesn't piss me off. What gets me mad, when you get loose.

Don What do you mean?

Teach You know what I mean.

Don No, I don't.

Teach Yes you do. I come in here. The kid's here.

Don He doesn't know anything.

Teach He doesn't.

Don No.

Teach What was he here for, then?

Don Sell me the buffalo.

Teach Sell it tonight.

Don Yeah.

Teach A valuable nickel.

Don We don't know.

Pause.

Teach Where is Fletch?

Don I don't know. (*Picks up phone and dials.*)

Teach He's not home. He's not home, Don. He's out.

Don (*into phone*) Hello?

Teach He's in?

Don This is Donny Dubrow.

Teach The Riv?

Don I'm looking for Fletcher.

Pause.

Okay. Thank you. (*He hangs up.*)

Teach Cocksucker should be horsewhipped with a horsewhip.

Don He'll show up.

Teach Fucking Riverside, too. (Thirty-seven cents for takeout coffee . . .)

Don Yeah. (*Picks up phone.*)

Teach A lot of nerve you come in there for sixteen years. This is not free enterprise.

Don No.

Teach You know what is free enterprise?

Don No. What?

Teach The freedom . . .

Don . . . yeah?

Teach Of the *Individual* . . .

Don . . . yeah?

Teach To Embark on Any Fucking Course that he sees fit.

Don Uh-huh . . .

Teach In order to secure his honest chance to make a profit. Am I so out of line on this?

Don No.

Teach Does this make me a Commie?

Don No.

Teach The country's *founded* on this, Don. You know this.

Don Did you get a chance to take a nap?

Teach Nap nap nap nap nap. Big deal.

Don (*pause*) Yeah.

Teach Without this we're just savage shitheads in the wilderness.

Don Yeah.

Teach Sitting around some vicious campfire. That's why *Ruthie* burns me up.

Don Yeah.

Teach (Nowhere dyke . . .) And take those fuckers in the concentration camps. You think they went in there by *choice*?

Don No.

Teach They were *dragged* in there, Don . . .

Don . . . yeah.

Teach Kicking and screaming. *Gimme* that fucking phone.

Teach *grabs phone. Listens. Hangs up.*

He's not home. I say *fuck* the cocksucker.

Don He'll show up.

Teach You believe that?

Don Yes.

Teach Then you are full of shit.

Don Don't tell me that, Teach. Don't tell me I'm full of shit.

Teach I'm sorry. You want me to hold your hand? This is how you keep score. I mean, we're all here . . .

Don Just, I don't want that talk.

Teach Don . . . I talk straight to you 'cause I respect you. It's kickass or kissass, Don, and I'd be lying if I told you any different.

Don And what makes you such an authority on life all of a sudden?

Teach My life, Jim. And the way I've lived it.

Pause.

Don Now what does that mean, Teach?

Teach What does that mean?

Don Yes.

Teach What does that *mean*?

Don Yes.

Teach Nothing. Not a thing. All that I'm telling you, the shot is yours. It's one night only. Too many guys know. All I'm saying. Take your shot.

Don Who knows?

Teach You and me.

Don Yeah.

Teach Bob and Fletcher. Earl, the phone guy, Grace and Ruthie, maybe.

Don Grace and Ruth don't know.

Teach Who *knows* they know or not, all that I'm telling you, it's not always so clear what's going on. Like Fletcher and the pig iron, that time.

Don What was the shot on that?

Teach He stole some pig iron off Ruth.

Don (I *heard* that . . .)

Teach That's a fact. A fact stands by itself. And we must face the facts and act on them. You better wake up, Don, right now, or things are going to fall around your *head*, and you are going to turn around to find he's took the joint off by himself.

Don He would not do that.

Teach He would. He is an animal.

Don He don't have the address.

Teach He doesn't know it.

Don No.

Teach Now, that is wise. Then let us go and take what's ours.

Don We have a deal with the man.

Teach With Fletcher.

Don Yes.

Teach We had a deal with Bobby.

Don What does that mean?

Teach Nothing.

Don It don't.

Teach No.

Don What did you mean by that?

Teach I didn't mean a thing.

Don You didn't.

Teach No.

Don You're full of shit, Teach.

Teach I am.

Don Yes.

Teach Because I got the balls to face some facts?

Pause.

You scare me sometimes, Don.

Don Oh, yeah?

Teach Yes. I don't want to go around with you here, things go down, we'll settle when we're done. We have a job to do here. Huh? Forget it. Let's go, come on.

Don We're waiting for him.

Teach Fletcher.

Don Yes.

Teach Why?

Don Many reasons.

Teach Tell me one. You give me one good reason, why we're sitting here, and I'll sit down and never say a word. One reason. One. Go on. I'm listening.

Don He knows how to get in.

Pause.

Teach Good night, Don. (*He starts to go for door.*)

Don Where are you going?

Teach Home.

Don You're going home.

Teach Yes.

Don Why?

Teach You're fucking with me. It's all right.

Don Hold on. You tell me how I'm fucking with you.

Teach Come on, Don.

Don You asked me the one reason.

Teach You make yourself ridiculous.

Don Yeah?

Teach Yeah.

Don Then answer it.

Teach What is the question.

Don Fletch knows how to get in.

Teach 'Get in.' That's your reason?

Don Yes.

Pause.

Teach What the fuck they live in Fort Knox? ('Get in.') (*Snorts.*) You break in a *window*, worse comes to worse you kick the fucking *back door* in. (What do you think this is, the Middle Ages?)

Don What about he's got a safe?

Teach Biiiig fucking deal.

Don How is that?

Teach You want to know about a safe?

Don Yes.

Teach What you do, a *safe* . . . you find the combination.

Don Where he wrote it down.

Teach Yes.

Don What if he didn't write it down?

Teach He wrote it down. He's *gotta* write it down. What happens he forgets it?

Don What happens he doesn't forget it?

Teach He's gotta forget it, Don. Human nature. The point being, even he *doesn't* forget it, *why* does he not forget it?

Don Why?

Teach 'Cause he's got it *wrote down*.

Pause.

That's why he *writes* it down.

Pause.

Huh? Not because he's some fucking turkey can't even remember the combination to his own *safe* . . . but only in the event that (God forbid) he somehow *forgets* it . . . he's got it wrote down.

Pause.

This is common sense.

Pause.

What's the good keep the stuff in the safe, every time he wants to get at it he's got to write away to the manufacturer?

Don Where does he write it?

Teach What difference? *Here* . . . We go in, I find the combination fifteen minutes, tops.

Pause.

There are only just so many places it could be. Man is a creature of habits. Man does not change his habits overnight. This is not like him. (And if he does, he has a very good reason.) Look, Don: You want to remember something (you write it down). Where do you put it?

Pause.

Don In my wallet.

Pause.

Teach *Exactly*!

Pause.

Okay?

Don What if he didn't write it down?

Teach He wrote it down.

Don I know he did. But just, I'm saying from *another* instance. Some made-up guy from my imagination.

Teach You're saying in the instance of some guy . . .

Don (Some *other* guy . . .)

Teach . . . he didn't write it down?

Pause.

Don Yes.

Teach Well, this is another thing.

Pause.

You see what I'm saying?

Don Yeah.

Teach It's another matter. The guy, he's got the shit in the safe, he didn't write it *down* . . .

Pause.

Don . . . ?

Don Yes?

Teach How do you know he didn't write it down?

Don (I'm, you know, making it up.)

Pause.

Teach Well, then, this is not based on *fact*.

Pause.

You see what I'm saying?

I can sit here and tell you *this*, I can tell you *that*, I can tell you any fucking thing you care to mention, but what is the point?

You aren't telling me he didn't write it down. All that you're saying, you can't *find* it. Which is only natural, as you don't know where to look. All I'm asking for a little trust here.

Don I don't know.

Teach Then you know what? Fuck you. (All day long. Grace and Ruthie Christ) What am I standing here convincing you? What am I doing demeaning myself standing here pleading with you to protect your best interests? I can't believe this, Don. Somebody told me I'd do this for you . . . (For *anybody*) I'd call him a liar. (I'm coming in here to efface myself.) I am not Fletch, Don, no, and you should thank God and fall *down* I'm not. (You're coming in here all the time that 'He's so good at cards . . .') The man is a cheat, Don. He *cheats* at cards – Fletcher, the guy that you're waiting for.

Don He cheats.

Teach Fucking A right, he does.

Don Where do you get this?

Pause.

You're full of shit, Walt. You're saying Fletch cheats at cards.

Pause.

You've seen him. You've *seen* him he cheats.

Pause.

You're *telling* me this?

Teach (The whatchamacallit is always the last to know.)

Don Come on, Walt, I mean, forget with the job and all.

Teach You live in a world of your own, Don.

Don Fletch cheats at cards.

Teach Yes.

Don I don't believe you.

Teach Ah. You can't take the truth.

Don No. I am sorry. I play in this fucking game.

Teach And you don't know what goes on.

Don I leave Fletcher alone in my *store*. . . . He could take me off any time, day and night.

What are you telling me, Walt? This is nothing but poison, I don't want to hear it. (*Pause.*)

Teach And that is what you say.

Don Yes. It is.

Pause.

Teach Think back, Donny. Last night. On one hand. You lost two hundred bucks.

Pause.

You got the straight, you stand pat. I go down before the draw.

Don Yeah.

Teach He's got what?

Don A flush.

Teach That is correct. How many did he take?

Don What?

Teach How many did he take?

Pause.

Don One?

Teach No. Two, Don. He took two.

Pause.

Don Yeah. He took two on that hand.

Teach He takes two on your standing pat, you kicked him thirty bucks? He draws two, comes out with a *flush*?

Don (*pause*) Yeah?

Teach And spills his fucking Fresca?

Don Yeah?

Teach Oh. You remember that?

Don (*pause*) Yeah.

Teach And we look down.

Don Yeah.

Teach When we look back, he has come up with a king-high flush.

Pause.

After he has drawed two.

Pause.

You're better than that, Don. You *knew* you had him beat, and you were right.

Pause.

Don It could happen.

Teach Donny . . .

Don Yeah?

Teach He laid down five red cards. A heart flush to the king.

Pause.

Don Yeah?

Teach I swear to God as I am standing here that when I threw my hand in when you raised me out, that I folded the king of hearts.

Pause.

Don You never called him out.

Teach No.

Don How come?

Teach (He don't got the address the guy?)

Don I told you he didn't.

Pause.

He's cheating, you couldn't say anything?

Teach It's not my responsibility, to cause bloodshed. I am not your keeper. You want to face facts, okay.

Don I can't believe this, Teach.

Teach (Friendship is marvelous.)

Don You couldn't say a word?

Teach I tell you now.

Don He was cheating, you couldn't say anything?

Teach Don. Don, I see you're put out, you find out this guy is a cheat . . .

Don According to you.

Teach According to me, yes I am the person it's usually according to when I'm talking. Have you noticed this? And I'm not crazed about it you're coming out I would lie to you on this. *Fuck* this. On anything. Wake up, Jim. I'm not the cheat. I know you're not mad at me, who are you mad at? Who fucked you up here, Don? Who's not here? Who?

Don Ruth knows he cheats?

Teach Who is the bitch in league with?

Don Him?

Teach (*pause*) You know how much money they took from this game?

Don Yeah?

Teach Well, I could be wrong.

Don Don't fuck with me here, Teach.

Teach I don't fuck with my friends, Don. I don't fuck with my business associates. I am a businessman, I am here to do business, I am here to face facts.

(Will you open your eyes . . . ?) The kid comes in here, he has got a certain coin, it's like the one *you* used to have . . . the guy you brought in doesn't show, we don't know where *he* is.

Pause.

Something comes down, some guy gets his house took *off*.

Pause.

Fletcher, he's not showing up. All right. Let's say I don't know why. Let's say *you* don't know why. But I know that we're both better off. We are better off, Don.

Pause.

What time is it?

Don It's midnight.

Pause.

Teach I'm going out there now. I'll need the address.

Teach *takes out revolver and begins to load it.*

Don What's that?

Teach What?

Don That.

Teach This 'gun'?

Don Yes.

Teach What does it look like?

Don A gun.

Teach It *is* a gun.

Don (*rises and crosses to center*) I don't like it.

Teach Don't look at it.

Don I'm serious.

Teach So am I.

Don We don't need a gun, Teach.

Teach I pray that we don't, Don.

Don We don't, tell me why we need a gun.

Teach It's not a question do we *need* it . . . *Need* . . . Only that it makes me comfortable, okay? It helps me to relax.

So, God forbid, something inevitable occurs and the choice is (And I'm *saying* 'God forbid') it's either him or us.

Don Who?

Teach The guy. I'm saying God forbid the *guy* (or somebody) comes in, he's got a knife . . . a cleaver from one of those magnetic *boards* . . . ?

Don Yeah?

Teach . . . with the two *strips* . . . ?

Don Yeah?

Teach And *whack*, and somebody is bleeding to death. This is all. Merely as a deterrent.

Pause.

All the preparation in the world does not mean *shit*, the path of some crazed lunatic sees you as an invasion of his personal domain. Guys go nuts, Don, *you* know this. Public *officials* . . . Ax murderers . . . all I'm saying, look out for your own.

Don I don't like the gun.

Teach It's a personal thing, Don. A personal thing of mine. A silly personal thing. I just like to have it along. Is this so unreasonable.

Don I don't want it.

Teach I'm not going without it.

Don Why do you want it?

Teach Protection of me and my partner. Protection, deterence. (We're only going around the fucking *corner* for Chrissake . . .)

Don I don't want it with.

Teach I can't step down on this, Don. I got to have it with. The light of things as they are.

Don Why?

Teach Because of the way *things* are. (*He looks out window.*) Hold on a second.

Don Fletcher?

Teach Cops.

Don What are they doing?

Teach Cruising.

Pause.

Don They turn the corner?

Teach Hold on.

Pause.

Yes.

They have the right idea. Armed to the hilt. Sticks, Mace, knives . . . who knows *what* the fuck they got. They have the right idea. Social customs break down, next thing *everybody's* lying in the gutter.

A knocking is heard at the door.

(Get down.) (Douse the light.)

Don (Lemme see who it is . . .)

Teach Don't answer it.

Bob (*from behind door*) Donny?

Teach (Great.)

Don (It's Bobby.)

Teach (I know.)

Bob Donny?

Pause.

Teach (Don't let him in.)

Don (He knows we're in here.)

Teach (So let him go away, then.)

Bob I got to talk to you.

Don *looks at* **Teach**.

Don (*to* **Bob**) What is it?

Bob I can't come in?

Teach (Get him outta here.)

Pause.

Don Bob . . .

Bob Yeah?

Don We're busy here.

Bob I got to talk to you.

Don *looks at* **Teach**.

Teach (Is he alone?)

Don (I think.)

Teach (*pause*) (Hold on.)

Teach *opens door and pulls* **Bob** *in.*

What, Bob? What do you want? You know we got work to do here, we don't need you to do it, so what are you doing here and what do you want?

Bob To talk to Don.

Teach Well, Don does not want to talk to you.

Bob I got to talk to him.

Teach You do not have to do anything, Bob. You do not have to do anything that we tell you that you have to do.

Bob I got to talk to Donny (*To* **Don**.) Can I talk to you? (*Pause. To* **Don**.) I came here . . .

Don . . . yeah?

Bob . . . The Riverside?

Don Yeah?

Bob Grace and Ruthie . . . he's in the hospital. Fletch.

Pause.

I only wanted to, like, *come* here. I know you guys are only playing *cards* this . . . now. I didn't want to disturb

you like *up*, but they just I found out he was in the
hospital and I came over here to . . . tell you.

Pause.

Teach With what?

Bob He got mugged.

Teach You're so full of shit.

Bob I think some Mexicans.

Teach *snorts*.

He did. He's in the hospital.

Teach You see this, Don?

Don He's mugged?

Bob Yeah, Grace, they just got back. They broke his jaw.

Teach They broke his jaw.

Bob Yeah. Broke.

Teach And now he's in the hospital. Grace and Ruthie
just got back. You thought that you'd come over.

Bob Yeah.

Teach Well, how about this, Don? Here Fletch is in
Masonic Hospital a needle in his arm, huh. How about
this?

Don How bad is he?

Bob They broke his jaw.

Don What else?

Bob I don't know.

Teach Would you believe this if I told you this this
afternoon?

Don When did it happen, Bob?

Bob Like before.

Don Before, huh?

Bob Yeah.

Teach How about this, Don?

Bob We're going to see him tomorrow.

Don When?

Bob I don't know. In the morning.

Don They got hours in the morning?

Bob I guess so.

Teach Hey, thanks for coming here. You did real good in coming here.

Bob Yeah?

Teach (*to* **Don**) He did real good in coming here, huh, Donny? (*To* **Bob**) We really owe you something.

Bob What for?

Teach Coming here.

Bob What?

Teach Something.

Bob Like what?

Don He don't know. He's saying that he thinks we owe you something, but right now he can't think what it is.

Bob Thanks, Teach.

Teach It's okay, Bob.

Pause. **Bob** *starts to exit.*

Stick around.

Bob Okay. For a minute.

Teach What? You're busy?

Bob I got, like, some things to do.

Teach Whaddaya got, a 'date'?

Bob No.

Teach What, then?

Bob Business.

Pause.

Don Where did they take him, Bob?

Pause.

Bob Uh, Masonic.

Don I don't think that they got hours start til after lunch.

Bob Then we'll go then. I'm gonna go now.

Teach Hold on a second, Bob. I feel we should take care of you for coming here.

Bob That's okay. I'll see you guys.

Don Come here a minute, Bobby.

Bob What, Donny?

Don What's going on here?

Bob Here?

Don Yes.

Pause.

Bob Nothing.

Don I'm saying what's happening, Bob?

Bob I don't know.

Don Where did you get that nickel from?

Bob What nickel?

Don You know what nickel, Bob, the nickel I'm talking about.

Bob I got it off a guy.

Don What guy?

Bob I met downtown.

Teach What was he wearing?

Bob Things.

Pause.

Don How'd you get it off him, Bob?

Bob We kinda talked.

Pause.

Don You know what, you look funny, Bob.

Bob I'm late.

Don It's after midnight, Bob. What are you late for?

Bob Nothing.

Don (*very sadly*) Jesus. Are you fucking with me here?

Bob No.

Don (Bobby.)

Bob I'm not fucking with you, Donny.

Pause.

Don Where's Fletcher?

Pause.

Bob Masonic.

Don *goes to telephone and dials information.*

Don (*into phone*) For Masonic Hospital, please.

Bob . . . I *think* . . .

Don (*to* **Bob**) What?

Bob He might not be Masonic.

Don (*to phone*) Thank you. (*Hangs up phone. To* **Bob**.) Now, *what*?

Bob He might not *be* there . . .

Don You said he was there.

Bob Yeah, I just, like, I *said* it. I really don't remember what they said, Ruthie.

Teach (Ruthie.)

Bob . . . so I just . . . *said* Masonic.

Don Why?

Bob I thought of it.

Pause.

Don Uh-huh. (*To phone*.) Yes. I'm looking for a guy was just admitted. Fletcher Post.

Pause.

Just a short time ago.

Pause.

Thank you. (*Pause. To* **Bob** *and* **Teach**.) She's looking for it. (*To phone*.) No?

Bob (I told you . . .)

Don You're sure?

Pause.

Thank you. (*Hangs up phone. To* **Bob**.) He's not there.

Bob I told you.

Teach (What did I tell you, Don?)

Don Where is he?

Teach Somewhere else.

Don (This makes me nuts . . .) Bobby . . .

Bob Yeah?

Pause.

They broke his jaw.

Don Who?

Bob Some spics. I don't know.

Teach *snorts.*

They did.

Don Who?

Teach Yeah?

Don Who is this 'they,' Bob, that you're talking about?

Teach Bob. . . .

Bob . . . yeah?

Teach Who are these people you're talking about?

Bob They broke his jaw.

Teach They took it in them all of a sudden they broke his jaw.

Bob They didn't care it was him.

Teach No?

Bob No, Teach.

Teach So who is it takes him out by accident. Huh? Grace and Ruthie?

Bob They wouldn't do that.

Teach I'm not saying they would.

Bob (*to* **Don**) What is he saying, Donny?

Teach Bob, Bob, Bob . . . what am I saying . . .

Pause.

Don Where's Fletch, Bobby?

Bob Hospital.

Teach Aside from that.

Bob All I know, that's the only place he is, Teach.

Teach Now, don't get smart with me, Bob, don't get smart with me, you young fuck, we've been sweating blood all day on this and I don't want your smart mouth on it (fuck around with Grace and Ruthie, and you come in here . . .), so all we want some answers. Do you understand?

Pause.

I told you: Do you understand this?

Don You better answer him.

Bob I understand.

Teach Then let's make *this* clear. Loyalty does not mean *shit* a situation like this; I don't know what you and them are up to, and I do not care, but only you come clean with us.

Bob He might of been a different hospital.

Teach Which one?

Bob *Any* of 'em.

Don So why'd you say 'Masonic'?

Bob I just thought of it.

Teach Okay. Okay . . . Bob?

Bob . . . yes?

Teach I want for you to tell us here and now (and for your own protection) what is going *on*, what is set *up* . . . where *Fletcher* is . . . and everything you know.

Don (*sotto voce*) (I can't believe this.)

Bob I don't know anything.

Teach You don't, huh?

Bob No.

Don Tell him what you know, Bob.

Bob I don't know it, Donny. Grace and Ruthie . . .

Teach *grabs a nearby object and hits* **Bob** *viciously on the side of the head.*

Teach Grace and Ruthie up your ass, you shithead; you don't fuck with us, *I'll* kick your fucking head in. (I don't give a shit . . .)

Pause.

You *twerp* . . .

A pause near the end of which **Bob** *starts whimpering.*

I don't give a shit. (Come in here with your fucking stories . . .

Pause.

Imaginary people in the hospital . . .

Bob *starts to cry.*

That don't mean shit to me, you fruit.

Bob Donny . . .

Don You brought it on yourself.

Teach Sending us out there . . . who the fuck knows what . . .

Bob He's in the hospital.

Don Which hospital?

Bob I don't know.

Teach Well, then, you better make one up, and quick.

Don Bob . . .

Teach (Don't back down on this, Don. Don't back down on me here.)

Don Bob . . .

Bob . . . yeah?

Don You got to see our point here.

Bob (*whimpering*) Yeah, I do.

Don Now, we don't want to hit you . . .

Teach (No.)

Bob I know you don't.

Teach No.

Don But you come in here . . .

Bob . . . yeah . . .

Don . . . the only one who knows the score . . .

Bob Yeah . . . (My ear is bleeding. It's coming out my ear.) Oh, fuck, I'm real scared.

Don (Shit.)

Bob I don't feel good.

Teach (Fuckin' kid poops out on us . . .)

Bob Don . . .

Teach Now what are we going to do with this?

Don You know, we didn't want to do this to you, Bob.

Bob I know . . .

Don We didn't want to do this.

Phone rings.

Teach (Great.)

Don (*to phone*) What? What the fuck do *you* want?

Teach (It's the guy?)

Don (*It's Ruthie.*) (*To phone.*) Oh yeah, we heard about that, Ruth.

Teach (*She's* got a lot of nerve . . .)

Don (*to phone*) From Bobby. Yeah. We'll *all* go.

Pause.

I thought he was at Masonic? Bobby. Well, okay, that's where we'll go then, Ruthie, we aren't going to go and see him at some hospital he isn't even *at* . . .

Pause.

Bobby's not here. I will. Okay. I will. Around eleven. Okay. (*He hangs up.*)

Teach (*to* **Bob**) And you owe me twenty bucks.

Don (*dialing*) For Columbus Hospital, please.

Teach (Fuckin' medical costs . . .)

Don Thank you.

Teach (*singing softly to himself*) '. . . and I'm never ever sick at sea.'

Don Yes. For Fletcher Post, please, he was just admitted?

Pause.

No. I only want to know is he all right, and when we go to see him.

Pause.

Thank you.

Teach What?

Don She's looking. (*To phone*) Yes? Yeah. Thank you very much. Yes. You've been very kind. (*He hangs up phone.*)

Teach What is he, *in* there?

Don Yeah.

Teach And they won't let us talk to him?

Don His jaw is broke.

Bob I feel funny.

Teach Your ear hurts.

Don Bob, it hurts. Bob?

Teach I never felt quite right on this.

Don Go tilt your head the other way.

Teach I mean, we're fucked up here. We have not blown the shot, but we're fucked up.

Don We are going to take you to the hospital.

Teach Yeah, yeah, we'll take you to the hospital, you'll get some care, this isn't a big deal.

Don Bob, you fell downstairs, you hurt your ear.

Teach He understands?

Don You understand? We're going to take you to the hospital, you fell downstairs.

Teach (*at door*) This fucking rain.

Don You give 'em your right name, Bob, and you know what you can tell 'em. (*Reaches in pocket, thrusts money at* **Bob**.) You hold on to this, Bob. Anything you want inside the hospital.

Bob I don't want to go to the hospital.

Teach You're going to the hospital, and that's the end of it.

Bob I don't want to.

Don You got to, Bob.

Bob Why?

Teach You're fucked up, that's why.

Bob I'm gonna do the job.

Don We aren't going to do the job tonight, Bob.

Teach You got a hat or something keep my head dry?

Don No.

Bob I get to do the job.

Teach You shut up. You are going to the hospital.

Don We aren't going to do the job tonight.

Bob We do it sometime else.

Don Yeah.

Teach He ain't going to do no job.

Don Shut up.

Teach Just say he isn't going to do no job.

Don It's done now.

Teach What?

Don I'm saying, this is over.

Teach No, it's not, Don. It is not. He does no job.

Don You leave the fucking kid alone.

Teach You want kids, you go have them. *I* am not your wife. *This* doesn't mean a thing to me. *I'm* in this. And it *isn't* over. This is for me, and this is my question:

Pause.

Where did you get that coin?

Bob What?

Teach Where'd you get that fucking nickel, if it all comes out now.

Pause.

He comes in here, a fifty dollars for a nickel, where'd you get it?

Bob Take me to the hospital.

Pause.

Teach Where did you get that nickel? (I want you to watch this.)

Pause.

Bob I bought it.

Teach (Mother Fucking Junkies.)

Don Shut up.

Teach What are you saying that you bought that coin?

Bob Yeah.

Teach Where?

Bob A coin store.

Pause.

Teach You bought it in a coin store.

Bob Yeah.

Pause.

Teach Why?

Don Go get your car.

Teach What did you pay for it?

Pause.

What did you pay for it?

Bob Fifty dollars.

Teach You buy a coin for fifty dollars, you come back here.

Pause.

Why?

Don Go get your fucking car.

Teach Why would you do a thing like that?

Bob I don't know.

Teach Why would you go do a thing like that?

Bob For Donny.

Pause.

Teach You people make my flesh crawl.

Don Bob, we're going to take you out of here.

Teach I can not take this anymore.

Don Can you walk?

Bob No.

Don Go and get your car.

Teach I am not your nigger. I am not your wife.

Don I'm through with you today.

Teach You are.

Don Yes.

Teach Why?

Pause.

Don You have lamed this up real good.

Teach I did.

Don Real good.

Teach I lamed it up.

Bob He hit me.

Don I know, Bob.

Teach Yes, I hit him. For his own good. For the good of all.

Don Get out of here.

Teach 'Get out of here'? And now you throw me out like *trash*? I'm doing this for *you*. What do I have to wreck this joint *apart*? He told you that he bought it in a *coin store*.

Don I don't care.

Teach You don't *care*? (I cannot believe this.) You *believe* him?

Don I don't *care*. I don't *care* anymore.

Teach You *fake*. You fucking *fake*. You fuck your friends. You *have* no friends. No *wonder* that you fuck this kid around.

Don You shut your mouth.

Teach You seek your friends with *junkies*. You're a joke on this street, you and him.

Don Get out.

Teach I do not go out, no.

Bob (I eat shit.)

Don You get out of here.

Teach I am not going anywhere. I have a piece of this.

Don You have a piece of *shit*, you fucking lame. (*Advancing on him.*)

Teach (This from a man who has to buy his friends.)

Don *I'll* tell you friends, *I'll* give you friends . . . (*Still advancing.*)

Bob (Oh, fuck . . .)

Don The stinking deals you come in here . . .

Teach You stay away from me . . .

Don You stiff this one, you stiff that one . . . you come in here, you stick this poison in me . . . (*hitting him*).

Teach (Oh, Christ . . .)

Bob (I eat shit.)

Teach (Oh, my God, I live with madmen.)

Don All these years . . .

Bob (All cause I missed him.)

Don (*advancing again*) All these fucking years . . .

Teach (You're going to hit me.)

Bob Donny . . .

Don You make life of garbage.

Bob Donny!

Teach (Oh, my God.)

Bob I missed him.

Don (*stopping*) What?

Bob I got to tell you what a fuck I am.

Don What?

Bob I missed him.

Don Who?

Bob The guy.

Don What guy?

Bob The guy this morning.

Don What guy?

Bob With the suitcase.

Don (*pause*) You missed him?

Bob I eat shit.

Don What are you saying that you lied to me?

Bob I eat shit.

Teach What is he saying?

Pause.

Don You're saying that you lied?

Teach What is he saying?

Don You're saying you didn't see him with the suitcase?

Teach This kid is hysterical.

Don You didn't see him?

Teach He's saying that he didn't see him?

Don When he left this morning.

Teach He's saying that he lied?

Bob I'm going to throw up.

Teach He's saying he didn't see the guy?

Pause.

When he came out, I was in here. *Then* you saw him.
When he had the suitcase. (*Pause.*) Then.

Pause.

You saw him *then*.

Pause. **Bob** *shakes his head.*

My Whole Cocksucking Life.

Teach *picks up the dead-pig sticker and starts trashing the junkshop.*

The Whole Entire World.

There Is No Law.

There Is No Right And Wrong.

The World Is Lies.

There Is No Friendship.

Every Fucking Thing.

Pause.

Every God-forsaken Thing.

Don Calm down, Walt.

Teach We all live like the cavemen.

During the speech, **Don** *tries to subdue* **Teach**, *and finally does.*

Don (Siddown.)

Pause.

Teach *sits still.*

Teach I went on a limb for you.

Pause.

You don't know what I go through. I put my dick on the chopping block.

Pause.

I hock my fucking watch . . .

Pause.

I go out there. I'm out there every day.

Pause.

There is nothing out there.

Pause.

I fuck myself.

Pause.

Don Are you all right?

Teach What?

Don Are you all right.

Teach How the fuck do I know?

Don You tire me out, Walt.

Teach What?

Don I need a rest.

Teach This fucking day.

Don (*pause*) My shop's fucked up.

Teach I know.

Don It's all fucked up.

Pause.

You fucked my shop up.

Teach Are you mad at me?

Don What?

Teach Are you mad at me?

Pause.

Don Come on.

Teach Are you?

Don Go and get your car. Bob?

Teach (*pause*) Tell me are you mad at me.

Don No.

Teach You aren't?

Don No.

Pause.

Teach Good.

Don You go and get your car.

Teach You got a hat?

Don No.

Teach Do you have a piece of paper?

Don Bob . . . ?

Teach *walks to counter, takes a piece of newspaper, and starts making himself a paper hat.*

Teach He's all right?

Don Bob . . . ?

Teach Is he all right?

Don Bob . . . ?

Bob (*waking up*) What?

Don Come on. We're taking you the hospital.

Teach *puts on paper hat and looks at self in window.*

Teach I look like a sissy.

Don Go and get your car.

Pause.

Teach Can you get him to the door?

Don Yeah.

Pause.

Teach I'm going to get my car.

Don You gonna honk?

Teach Yeah.

Don Good.

Teach I'll honk the horn.

Pause.

Don Good.

Pause.

Teach This fucking day, huh?

Don Yeah.

Teach I know it. You should clean this place up.

Don Yeah.

Pause.

Teach Good. (*Exits.*)

Don Bob.

Bob What?

Don Get up.

Pause.

Bob. I'm sorry.

Bob What?

Don I'm sorry.

Bob I fucked up.

Don No. You did real good.

Bob No.

Don Yeah. You did real good.

Pause.

Bob Thank you.

Don That's all right.

Pause.

Bob I'm sorry, Donny.

Don That's all right.

Lights dim.

The Water Engine

An American Fable

'The mind of man is less perturbed by a mystery he cannot explain than by an explanation he cannot understand.'
— Lenox Lohr, General Manager,
The Century of Progress Exposition

The Water Engine was first written as a radio play for Earplay, for National Public Radio. The stage version was first produced by the St. Nicholas Theatre Company, Chicago, Illinois, May 11, 1977, with the following cast:

Charles Lang	W. H. Macy
Rita	Gail Silver
Martin Keegan (Morton Gross)	Michael O'Dwyer
Lawrence Oberman	Guy Barile
Mrs Varĕc	Belinda Bremner
Mr Wallace	Norm Tobin
Bernie	Joseph Weisberg
Dave Murray	Dan Conway

Directed by Steven Schachter

The New York Shakespeare Festival Public Theatre production of *The Water Engine* produced by Joseph Papp opened on January 5, 1978, in New York City, with the following cast:

Charles Lang	Dwight Schultz
Rita	Penelope Allen
Morton Gross	David Sabin
Lawrence Oberman	Bill Moor
Mrs Varĕc	Barbara Tarbuck
Mr Wallace	Dominic Chianese
Bernie	Michael J. Miller
Dave Murray	Colin Stinton

Directed by Steven Schachter

The Water Engine, produced by Joseph Papp, opened at the Plymouth Theatre on Broadway on March 6, 1978, New York City, with the following cast:

Charles Lang	Dwight Schultz
Rita	Patti LuPone
Morton Gross	David Sabin
Lawrence Oberman	Bill Moor
Mrs Varĕc	Barbara Tarbuck
Mr Wallace	Dominic Chianese
Bernie	Michael J. Miller
Dave Murray	Colin Stinton

Directed by Steven Schachter

The Water Engine received its British première on 21 August 1989 at the Hampstead Theatre, London with the following cast:

Charles Lang	Peter Whitman
Rita	Mary Maddox
Morton Gross	Peter Jonfield
Lawrence Oberman	Nick Dunning
Mrs Varěc	Michelle Newell
Mr Wallace	Malcolm Terris
Bernie	Aiden Gillen
Dave Murray	Stephen Boxer
Chain Letter	David Healey

Directed by Robin Lefèvre

The Water Engine is set in a radio station studio in 1934.

Act One

Cast members gather at the microphone and sing.

Singers
'By the rivers gently flowing,
Illinois, Illinois
Lie thy praries verdant growing
Illinois, Illinois
Til upon thine Island Sea
Stands Chicago, great and free,
Turning all the world to thee,
Illinois, Illinois.'

Announcer (*voice over*) . . . aaand welcome to The
Century of Progress Exposition. Yes, the Second Hundred
Years of Progress. (*Pause.*) The concrete poetry of
Humankind. Much is known and much will yet be known.
As we rush on.

Chicago, 1934. The Century of Progress

Lang *in his laboratory.*

Lang The techniques of chemistry should not be difficult.
We are all made of chemicals. We are the world in this
respect. (*Pause.*) Things can work out. Things can work
out if we will persevere. (*Pause.*) If we will think correctly.
Why must I distinguish between inorganic and organic?
All things come from hydrogen. They all come from the
earth. As we do. We are made of molecules. We all are
made of light. We are the world in this respect.

At the Chicago Daily News. *Newspaper sounds.*

Murray Boy.

Boy Yessir.

Murray Run this down to the composing room.

Boy Yessir.

Murray Hold on. (*Pause.*) I want to ask you something. 'Were it left to me to decide whether we should have a government without newspapers, or newspapers without a government, I should not hesitate to prefer the latter.' (*Pause.*) Do you know who said that?

Boy No, Mr Murray.

Murray Good.

Secretary You done?

Murray Yeah. I'm done.

Secretary You want some breakfast?

Murray Yeah.

Secretary Come on.

Chain Letter (*voice over*) Neither the Rain nor Snow nor Gloom of Night stays these couriers from the swift completion of their appointed rounds.

At the candy store. Doorbell jingling.

Mr Wallace Bernie.

Bernie Yeah, Pop.

Mr Wallace See who just came in.

Mailman Mailman! Anybody want a letter?

Chain Letter (*voice over*) Do not break the chain.

Bernie It's only the mailman, Pop.

Mr Wallace Hey, Bernie, come here. What did I tell you?

Bernie What?

Mr Wallace When we close up at night we open up the register.

Bernie I'm sorry. (*Pause.*)

Mr Wallace Do you know why? (*Pause.*)

Bernie Yes, I'm sorry.

At **Morton Gross***' office.*

Secretary (*on phone*) Mr Gross' office . . . (*Pause.*) No. He's in conference.

Chain Letter (*voice over*) Many great and near-great men received this letter. Stanford White received this letter fifteen days before his murder.

Charles H. Lindbergh had received a copy just three days before the kidnapping. Both broke the chain.

Secretary (*to recalcitrant inventor in the waiting room*) Sit down, please.

Chain Letter (*voice over*) Pass this letter on to three friends. Happiness and health will be yours. One man in Montana received upwards of six thousand dollars. General Burchard in the Philippines received eleven thousand dollars but he lost his life because he broke the chain.

Secretary Sit down, please.

Postal Processor Inventor I want to talk to Mr Gross about a patent.

Lang *enters office.*

Secretary Yes?

Lang My name is Lang.

Secretary You have an appointment?

Lang Yes.

Secretary One minute.

Chain Letter (*voice over*) Do not break the chain.

Secretary You may go in.

Lang Thank you.

Chain Letter (*voice over*) In September, 1934, a young man in Chicago, Illinois designed and built an engine which used distilled water as its only fuel.

Gross Sit down. Sit down.

Lang Thank you.

Gross You are?

Lang Charles Lang.

Gross Glad to meet you.

Secretary (*on phone*) He's in Conference.

Gross Well, what can I do for you?

Lang I want to patent something.

Gross What?

Lang An engine.

Chain Letter (*voice over*) Write in *your* name at the bottom of the list. Send a postal order for one dollar to the name which appears at the top of the list, and cross that name off the list.

Gross Okay, good, tell me about it.

Lang First we should form an agreement.

Gross What?

Lang First we should form an agreement. If I give you money then we have a contract.

Gross You give me a dollar and that's a retainer and that constitutes a contract. Is that what you're saying?

Lang Yes.

Gross Then you can trust me. Is that what you're saying?

Lang Yes.

Gross Fine. Well, then give me a dollar.

Pause. **Lang** *hands* **Gross** *a dollar.*

Thank you. Do you trust me now? (*Pause.*) And if you couldn't trust me what good would your contract be?

Lang Well . . .

Gross What?

Lang There is a way things are.

Gross All right. (*Pause.*) Fine. Tell me about your invention. (*Pause.*)

Lang We have a contract now?

Gross (*sighs*) Mr Lang, you're what, you're a designer. I am an attorney, this is what I do, all right? Life is too short. Let's see what we can do for one another here?

Lang We have a contract?

Gross Yes. We have a contract. (*Pause.*)

Lang I want a patent for my engine.

Gross On what basis? (*Pause.*) What makes it special? (*Pause.*)

Lang It uses water for its only fuel. (*Pause.*) It runs on water. (*Pause.*)

Gross Who sent you here?

Lang I saw your name in the telephone directory.

Gross No. Who sent you here? Did Jimmy Dwyer at Henrici's send you here?

Lang I saw your name in the directory.

Gross You did.

Lang It turns out eight horsepower.

Secretary (*over intercom*) The man with the postal processor is back.

Gross Tell him no. (*Pause.*) Who are you?

Lang Charles Lang.

Gross You show me, Mr Lang, an engine that can run on water. Show me that. An engine cannot run on water, Mr Lang.

Lang I've freed the hydrogen. There's hydrogen in water?

Gross Yes.

Lang My engine runs on it.

Gross It does.

Lang Yes. You can see it.

Gross I can.

Lang In my laboratory. (*Pause.*)

Gross And you found my name in the phonebook.

Lang Yes. (*Gives him a paper.*) If you will come this evening you can see it. But I'm . . .

Gross What.

Lang I'm going to go to someone else if you don't come.

Gross (*smiling*) I thought we had a contract?

Lang I'll be there this evening.

Inventor I know that he's in there. I can hear him.

Lang (*leaving*) I'll be there this evening.

Inventor You gave me an appointment.

Secretary No, I certainly did not.

Inventor What must I *do*.

Lang *has left.*

Gross (*over intercom*) What have I got on this evening?

Secretary K. of C. (*Pause.*)

Gross Cancel it.

Inventor Please. May I go in?

Secretary No, will you go away. Will you please go away?

Inventor *walks to where* **Lang** *is waiting at the elevator.*

Inventor He won't see me.

Lang Why?

Inventor He won't see me any more.

Lang Why?

Inventor He says he's seen me.

Elevator Operator Down.

Inventor (*whispers*) I could revolutionize the mails.

Elevator Operator Down?

Inventor The delivery of mails.

Lang *gets on elevator.*

Lang Down. Thank you.

Lady on Elevator . . . and Roosevelt had let him in his cell.

Lady 2 Who told you that?

Lady My cousin.

Lady 2 How does she know?

Lady Well, her brother worked there.

Lady 2 At the prison?

Lady No, the paper.

Lady 2 And he let him in his cell?

Lady Yes.

Lady 2 Lindbergh?

Lady Yes. He told her that the Warden said that Lindbergh was allowed to be alone with him until the execution and whatever he wanted to do with him was fine.

Lady 2 No.

Lady Just as long as he lived.

Elevator Operator Five.

Lady 2 And so what did he do to him?

Lady They handcuffed him to the bars.

Lady 2 No.

Lady Yes. And then Lindbergh came in with this *Doctor's* bag . . .

Lady 2 No.

Lady . . . and they put up these curtains, and left him alone with Hauptman.

Lady 2 No.

Lady Until the execution.

Lady 2 And he chained him to the bars?

Lady Yes. And that's why they didn't allow the photographers.

Lady 2 You know, I *wondered* about that.

Elevator Operator Ground.

Lang Where is your telephone?

Elevator Operator *points.* **Lang** *leaves elevator.*

Lady And he was hardly breathing when they pulled the switch.

Lang (*on phone in lobby*) How are you?

Rita (*on phone*) I'm all right. (*Pause.*) Is he going to come?

Lang I think so.

Elevator Operator This car up.

Rita He wouldn't say?

Lang No.

Rita Did you tell him, just the way we worked it out?

Lang Yes. I think he'll come.

Rita You have to watch yourself.

Lang I know.

Elevator Operator Up.

Rita You must watch yourself.

Lang I know.

Elevator Operator We're going up.

Rita You don't. You must be careful. You don't know these people, Charles.

Lang I will be careful. (*Pause.*) I promise. (*Pause.*) How are you?

Rita I am fine. (*Pause.*)

Lang Is there anything that I can get you?

Rita No. (*Pause.*)

Lang I will see you later.

Rita Yes. You must be careful with these people.

Lang I will.

She hangs up. Hold. He hangs up. A knock is repeated.

Rita Who is it?

Mrs Varěc Mrs Varěc. (*Pause.*)

Rita Who?

Mrs Varěc Mrs Varěc. From upstairs.

Rita Oh yes, hello.

Mrs Varěc I'm going to the store. (*Pause.*) Can I get you something from the store? (*Pause.*)

Rita No thank you. (*Pause.*) Mrs Varěc, have a nice day.

Mrs Varěc And you too.

Mr Wallace *at his store, behind the counter.* **Lang** *and* **Bernie** *working on a toy airplane.*

Mr Wallace You wanna nother cup of coffee?

Lang No. No thank you, Mr Wallace.

Mr Wallace Do you want a doughnut?

Lang No.

Bernie Why don't we try to hook it to the aileron?

Lang All right, let's try.

Mr Wallace You seen that thing that they have over at the Fair the Hall of Science?

Lang What's that, Mr Wallace?

Mr Wallace The 'Rocket Ship.'

Lang No.

Bernie Could I please have the pliers?

Lang *hands him pliers.*

Bernie Thank you.

Mr Wallace Some of the things there, I cannot believe that they've got in the Future.

Bernie They're not only in the Future, Poppa.

Mr Wallace No?

Bernie Uh-*uh*, they've got 'em *now*.

Mr Wallace Yeah. Have you seen that at the Fair there, Mr Lang? The 'Rocket Ship'?

Lang No.

Mr Wallace You should go.

Lang I went last year.

Bernie I think I've got it. Mr Lang!

Mr Wallace It's not as good as last year.

Bernie See!

Lang Bernie, you're absolutely right.

Mr Wallace One thing that I like, though (*Pauses.*) the Hall of Science.

Lang You've got a good mind for mechanics, Bernie.

Mr Wallace 'A good mind for mechanics'! He's another Steinmetz!

Bernie Thank you, Mr Lang.

Mr Wallace *If* he applies himself.

Gross walks into store.

Mr Wallace Yessir?

Gross I'm here to meet *him*.

Lang I'll see you later, Bernie, Mr Wallace . . .

Mr Wallace Goodnight, Mr Lang, that's fifteen cents.

Lang hands him the money.

Mr Wallace Thank you.

Bernie Goodnight, Mr Lang.

Lang Goodnight, Bernie, you keep working.

Gross *and* **Lang** *exit.*

Mr Wallace So you fixed your airplane?

Bernie Yes.

Mr Wallace Good. (*Musing.*) The 'Rocket Ship' . . . some of those things in the Future I cannot believe.

Bernie They're not just in the Future, Poppa.

Mr Wallace No?

Bernie Uh-*uh*. They've got 'em *now*, they're right there at the Fair, they've got 'em *now*.

Mr Wallace They do?

Bernie Yes.

Mr Wallace Oh, and what makes you so smart? (*Pause.*) Let's close up.

Gross (*outside*) Well, here we are.

Lang Yes.

Gross Where are we going?

Lang Not far.

Gross You live around here?

Lang Not far.

Gross I looked you up.

Lang You did?

Gross Yes, I know where you live.

Lang Yes?

Gross We aren't going there.

Lang No. (*Pause.*)

Gross Well, that's all right, that's fine. (*Pause.*) Tell me how many people know. About this thing of yours.

Lang A friend and I. (*Pause.*) Me and a friend. You.

Gross I checked up on you.

Lang Yes.

Gross I spoke to your company. (*Pause.*) Dietz.

Lang How long do you think it will take us to receive a patent?

Gross That depends.

Lang On what?

Gross On many things. (*Pause.*) Do you want to know what they said?

Lang At my company?

Gross Yes.

Lang No. (*Pause.*) This is it.

They go into an alley and into **Lang**'s *laboratory.*

Gross My god. Who paid for all this?

Lang Sit down.

Gross This is all yours?

Lang Yes. Sit down.

Gross All of this equipment?

Lang Please don't touch that. (*Pause.*) This is my engine and this is water.

Gross Uh-huh.

Lang It's distilled. It won't be necessary in the end, but 'til I solve the carburation it's much cleaner. (*Starts to fuel machine.*)

Gross Yeah. Now can I taste that please? (*Does so.*)

Lang *proceeds to fix engine.*

Lang They told you what I do there.

Gross At the factory.

Lang Yes.

Gross Yes.

Lang Why did you come, then?

Gross We have a contract. What's that?

Lang Just a battery. I use electric charge for the ignition.

Gross All right.

Lang I'm going to start it now.

Gross Yeah. Wait. (*Patting pocket.*) You got a cigarette?

Lang No. What you're going to see is like a sailboat. My sister says. There are no more factories. This engine. (*Pause.*) This engine, Mr Gross, draws from the Earth. It draws its powers from the Earth. (*Pause. Preparation.*) Now: (*Touches spark. Nothing happens.*)

Gross What's the trouble? (*Pause.*)

Lang Nothing. We um, this is all right. Hold on one second. Wait. (*Makes a slight adjustment.*) (*Pause.*) Wait. (*Fiddles.*) All right. (*Touches spark. Nothing happens. Touches spark again. They sit there.*) I can fix this.

Gross (*getting up.*) Jimmy Dwyer at Henrici's sent you. You tell Jimmy, no, no. I'll tell Jimmy. This is wonderful. (*Laughing.*) 'I'm gonna be rich.' (*Exiting, laughing.*) Who are you, by the way?

Sound. Engine sparks, and bursts into life. They stand there.

Lang There are no more factories.

Chain Letter (*voice over*) . . . and, delayed by the storm she missed the evening mail by seconds.

The woman then ran on after the mail truck, letter in her hand and the postman saw her in the rearview mirror.

Driving home she found her house had been struck down by lightning.

Had she been there just one minute previously she would have perished in the fire.

Remember to enclose a postal order in the sum of One Dollar.

Make the order out in favor of the person whose name appears at the top of the list.

Lang *and* **Rita** *at the apartment. A radio dance band is heard beneath their conversation.*

Rita You know what I want?

Lang No.

Rita A place with a balcony. We can sit out.

Lang Yes.

Rita And feel the breeze. (*Pause.*) And fans. (*Pause.*) Electric fans.

Lang We're going to move from here.

Rita Where?

Lang The country.

Rita Good. (*Pause.*) We could have a farm.

Lang Have you been on a farm?

Rita Yes. And dogs. We could raise dogs. (*Pause.*) When are you meeting with him?

Lang Tomorrow night.

Rita Why at night? (*Pause.*)

Lang He said we must all be careful.

Rita Yes, we must. (*Pause.*) Do you trust him?

Lang No.

Rita They all are thieves, you know.

Lang Who?

Rita All of them are thieves. You moved the engine, didn't you?

Lang After he left.

Rita Good. And a windmill. We can sit out in the evening and we'll hear it go around . . . We'll hear it go around.

Lang Yes.

Rita Are you tired?

Lang Yes. I am.

Rita Don't trust him.

Lang No. I don't.

Radio Announcer (*voice over*) This concludes another evening of 'The Music That You Love To Dance To,' coming to you from Chicago's Famed Aragon Ballroom on the Great North Side. Until next Wednesday at this time, then, this is Arthur Riddle wishing you Good Night, Good Luck, and very pleasant dreams.

Rita *turns off the radio, silencing the* **Announcer.**

Chain Letter (*voice over*) The terror of the Cities of the Night is Stilled Commerce. Demons and the fears of sleep have been eradicated by the watchmen of the modern order. Now we are characters within a dream of industry. Within a dream of toil . . .

Lang *is seen at his factory working his punch press.*

Worker The unit boss come down here.

Lang He did.

Worker Ask the foreman where you were.

Lang What did he want?

Worker He wanted *you*. (*Pause.*) You know why?

Lang No.

Worker I know why.

Lang You do.

Worker Yeah. (*Pause.*) You watch yourself. (*Whistle blows.*)

Foreman Lunch!!!

On which note we leave the factory.

A Voice If a man worked all his life And put his life savings into dollars And he put them in a bag. And someone took it from him. Then where would he be? (*Pause.*) Had he not worked? Must he seek charity? (*Pause.*) The man who took it – When he spent it – Who would know it was not his?

In Bughouse Square. There are speakers, passers-by, hecklers, etc.

Soapbox Speaker . . . and every time I feel a thrill of pride . . .

Bum You got a smoke, pal, for a Vet?

Lang I'm sorry. What?

Soapbox Speaker When Patriotic Songs are played . . .

Bum You got a cigarette?

Lang No.

Soapbox Speaker And when Old Glory takes the breeze . . .

Lang Do you know what time it is?

Bum No.

Lang (*to another watcher*) Do you know what time it is?

Watcher No.

Soapbox Speaker I find myself ashamed. (*Pause.*) Yes. Ashamed. When will we learn to choose between the quality of our impressions? (*Pause.*)

*The **Soapbox Speaker** and the **Bum** speak simultaneously.*

Soapbox Speaker Patriotism is a real feeling. Yes. We feel it there beneath our breastbones, in our hearts, our spirits rise. It serves the cause of death.

Bum This man is good. I hear the things he's saying. I know what he's saying.

*The **Soapbox Speaker** continues to speak. **Lang** and **Mr Gross** converse simultaneously.*

Soapbox Speaker What is there so attractive in these tearful, pomp-filled ceremonies? What is so seductive in them? They support the torture of the ages. The Great War, the pogroms, the Crusades, the Inquisition (may God Bless us all) 'My Country Right or Wrong' – in nomine patri, fillii, spiritiis sancti. Let us go and free the Holy Land, The Maine, The Belgian Orphans . . .

Gross Lang. (*Pause.*) Lang.

Lang Are you late?

Gross What?

Lang Are you late?

Gross No. (*Pause.*)

Lang I was worried.

Gross Come on.

Lang Where?

Gross Around the corner. (*Pause.*) Come on.

Watcher Go back to Russia. (*This line should be spoken after the **Soapbox Speaker** says '. . . the pogroms, the Crusades. . . .'*)
Watcher I was there. Were you?

Soapbox Speaker Yes. And if I was not? (*Pause.*) We support these things, friend, you and I. The power of the torturers comes from the love of Patriotic Songs. We are the Hun.

Watcher Go back to Russia.

Soapbox Speaker Russia is a fiction, friend. She is a bugaboo inventor to distract you from your troubles. (*Pause.*) There is no Russia. Russia is the bear beneath your bed.

Gross How are you?

Lang I'm fine.

Gross Good.

Lang Where are we going?

Gross Not far. Do you ever come here?

Lang Bughouse Square?

Gross Yes.

Lang No.

Gross Well, I do. I like to hear the speeches. Get a different slant on things.

Lang Where are we going? (*Pause.*)

Gross I want you to meet someone.

Lang Who?

Gross A friend.

Lang Who is he?

Gross Someone who is going to help us. Here. (*Pause.*)

Oberman Mr Lang? (*Pause.*) Mr Lang? I'm very gland to meet you.

Gross This is Lawrence Oberman.

Lang Who are you?

Gross Charles, I'm going to stop back at my office.

Lang Who are you? Who is that man?

Gross A lawyer. A good friend of mine.

Lang A patent lawyer?

Gross Yes. I'm going back downtown.

Lang You're leaving.

Gross I have things to wrap up, Charles, don't worry. (*Pause.*) You're in the best of hands.

Lang You're leaving. (*Pause.*)

Gross I swear to you. You're in the best of hands. You take good care of him.

Oberman I will.

Gross I'll call you.

Oberman Call me in the morning.

Lang Wait. No. You must stay with me. (*Pause.*)

Gross Charles. (*Softly.*) Charles. I want you to stay here and talk to him.

Lang You stay with me.

Gross It isn't necessary. (*Pause.*) Really. It is not. Now, you come in tomorrow morning. Can you come in around ten?

Lang (*softly*) Yes.

Gross What?

Lang Yes.

Gross Then you come in then. (*Pause.*) (*To* **Oberman**.) And you take good care of him.

Oberman (*smiles*) I will.

Gross I know you will. (*To* **Lang**.) I'll see you in the morning. (*Exits.*)

Knife Grinder *walks through the neighborhood, and is heard softly singing.*

Knife Grinder Knives to grind. I've got your knives to grind. (*Pause.*) Knives to grind, I've got your knives to grind.

His song is heard and it fades beneath the following dialogue. **Lang** *and* **Oberman** *begin to walk.*

Oberman Well, how are you?

Lang Fine.

Oberman Good. (*Pause.*) Do you get up in the Park much?

Lang No.

Oberman Mmm.

Lang Not in years. (*Pause.*) Who are you?

Oberman I am a colleague of Morton's.

Lang You work with Gross?

Oberman Yes. I have.

Lang You are a lawyer.

Oberman Yes.

Lang For who? (*Pause.*) Who are you a lawyer for?

Oberman Well, Mr Lang, I hope that I will work for you. (*Pause.*)

Lang I have a lawyer.

Oberman (*smiles*) Mr Lang, I represent some interests which are very much concerned with this machine of yours. Now Gross thought, when he perceived the value of your engine, that it would be best for you quite quickly to avail yourself of aid. (*Pause.*) Specifically, of services which I am equipped to offer. (*Pause.*)

Lang What does that mean?

Oberman Listen to me. We wish to take your engine and develop and produce and market it in an economic and efficient a manner as possible; and in so doing make great profits for ourselves and you. (*Pauses. Smiles.*) That is what we want.

Lang You want to license it.

Oberman No, Mr Lang. We want to patent it. We want to buy it.

Lang (*pause*) Oh. (*Pause.*)

Oberman I should get up here more often.

Lang You want to buy it from me.

Oberman And we want to protect you.

Lang (*pause*) Protect me from what?

Oberman Shall we turn back here?

Lang Protect me from what?

Oberman (*sighs*) You needn't know. Come with us. See your engine made and utilized. (*Pause.*) Keep control of what you've made.

Lang I have control. It's mine.

Oberman The law is not precise on some points . . . litigation is expensive.

Lang If it isn't mine, whose is it? (*Pause.*) It's mine.

Oberman A substantial case could be made for the ownership of the machine by those who've paid for its development.

Lang And who is that?

Oberman (*pause*) Dietz and Federle. The company for

which you work. Shall we take one more turn around the block? They could say you had worked on the engine for many months while in their pay and on their premises. Now, you were forced by circumstances – as we know – to do this, and this is unfortunate. (*Pause.*) Perhaps more so was your . . . your decision to continue work on the machine at your own workshop. (*Pause.*) The laboratory you have built yourself on Halsted Street is fitted out entirely with tools and material from Dietz and Federle. Then to whom does the engine belong?

Lang I run a punchpress there. They pay me ninety cents an hour. I never stole a thing from them.

Oberman Now, Mr Lang, that just is not the truth. (*Pause.*) Let's not be specious. Everyone has motives, thieves included. They will say you are a thief, and they will be upheld.

Lang I made the engine.

Oberman Yes. God bless you. Yes. It is a work of genius. (*Pause.*) Whether you are able to establish ownership is quite another matter. (*Pause.*) Here we are. (*Smiles.*) Quite simply, Mr Lang, my people want the engine. Dietz would deal with us. We'd rather deal with you. But we will deal with whom we must. Will you entertain an offer for the right to patent the machine?

Lang Then you would own the engine.

Oberman Yes.

Lang No. I cannot accept that.

Oberman You know, you put us in an unprotected stance here. You do. (*Pause.*) By dealing with you a case could be made for our collusion in the theft.

Lang What theft?

Oberman Of the machine. I think that in the light of this our offer is – I am not going to tell you that it's generous

it may or may not be – but it is eminently reasonable.
(*Pause.*) Can you see that?

Lang I don't like you.

Oberman Let us not be romantic, Mr Lang. Sell us the
machine. I swear to you this offer is in your best interests.
Do you think I like conducting business in the park? In
darkness? You're in danger, Mr Lang. You are. And those
who deal with you are in danger. I know that you don't
believe this, but it's so. I swear to you. Sell us the engine.
(*Pause.*) You sleep on what we've talked about. Call me
tomorrow. Please. (*Pause.*)

Oberman *walks off. We hear the Bughouse Square* **Speaker**.

Speaker Where are the benefits to you and me? That's
what I say. Where are the benefits? A couple kids go off to
C.C.C., or build a bridge somewhere's, but what about
the Wheat? I ask you where's the Wealth, where is the
wealth? Now this is what I say. The ownership of land.
These things do not change. They don't change with
giveaways and murals. They are Bank Night at the
movies. That's all. That is all I have to say.

Crowd reaction.

Moderator Step down. Thank you. Anybody else would
like to speak? On any subject? Anybody?

At the apartment.

Rita Many cows and horses. All large animals need
constant care. You have to be with them if they are to be
productive. Sitting with them and just caring for their
needs. With sunshine. And with proper foods. You have to
get up early in the morning. When the sun is not up. All
the world smells like a bakery. Here. Here, my friends.
(*Pause.*) Here I am to help you.

Lang *enters the apartment.*

Rita Things can go wrong. You don't have to be down

when things go wrong, because each day is new. (*Pause.*)
Every day is new. Isn't it, Charley?

Lang Yes.

Rita When you can live out where it's clean. (*Pause.*)
When you're famous. (*Pause.*) Would you like something to
eat?

Lang I have to go back to the lab.

Rita Well, eat now. Cause I have to tell you what I'm
thinking.

Lang No. I have to move those things.

Rita Move them in the morning. Cause I have to tell you
things that I've been thinking about life here. (*Pause.*) You
move that stuff tomorrow. (*Pause.*)

Lang They said it wasn't mine.

Rita What wasn't yours?

Lang The engine. (*Pause.*)

Rita I miss the horses. All the horses. You remember, in
the street?

Lang Yes.

Rita The reason I don't like automobiles is fumes.

Lang They said it wasn't mine.

Rita Of course it's yours. Whose is it if it isn't yours? And
privacy. You can't keep things out. This is what I
thought: that when you live in here you can't control what
comes in. Sounds come in. And fumes. From things you
had no part in. (*Pause.*) Someone went down today. Down
on the fire escape. I think he stopped there by the
window. (*Pause.*) You can't control these things. (*Pause.*)
That's why every one should live out in the country. Don't
you think so?

Lang Yes.

Rita Where, if you have the money, you can use it to get back the things you need. (*Pause.*) Do you see?

Lang Yes.

Rita Good. What would you like to eat?

Lang I have to go back to the lab.

Rita No. You can go tomorrow. (*Pause.*) I think you're tired. You rest now. (*Pause.*) You stay with me now. (*Pause.*) The important thing is see it made. We'll see the engine made.

Lang We'll see the engine made.

Rita Yes. That's the only thing. And we'll have no machines.

Lang No.

Rita On our farm.

Lang No.

Rita Some machine. (*Pause.*) Very few. (*Pause.*) Very few machines.

Chain Letter (*voice over*) A Russian Prince, deposed and penniless in Paris sent the letter on, and two weeks later saw an advertisement in the local paper placed there by his long-lost brother whom he thought was dead.

The brother sought some information of the Prince's whereabouts; and he received his just inheritance at last.

An older woman who had been a nurse discovered fifty thousand dollars in a trunk which she had purchased at a railroad auction.

A missionary, deep in China, received a telegram which said his fiancée had died. The last act of his life prior to entering a monastery was to pass the letter on.

Fifteen years later . . .

Railroad Conductor (*announcing a train.*) For Buffalo . . . Rochester . . . Syracuse . . . Albany . . . 125th Street, and

Grand Central Station on Track Five. This is the
Twentieth Century Limited. On Track Five.

Lang *storms into* **Gross***'s office.*

Secretary One moment, Sir, he's with a client. *Sir* . . .

Lang (*to* **Gross**) Get up.

Secretary I'm sorry, Mr Gross, he . . .

Gross Close the door, please. (**Secretary** *retires.*) What's
the matter?

Lang Get up.

Gross Charles, what's the matter?

Lang You stand up, you punk.

Oberman, *who has been at the back of the office, speaks.*

Oberman Mr Lang . . .

Lang You, too. You people make me sick.

Gross Will you sit down, please? Why don't you sit
down?

Lang *stands for a moment, he dashes some object to the floor.*
Secretary *buzzes.*
Oberman *and* **Gross** *speak simultaneously.*

Oberman Are you in control now?

Gross (*into intercom*) No, it's nothing.

Oberman Are you all right now? (*Pause.*)

Gross Charles, what is it?

Oberman Can you tell us what's happening, Mr Lang?

Lang You're funny. (*Pause.*)

Gross What is it, Charles?

Lang You didn't know what's in there. You don't know.

If you cannot have it, *kill* it. (*Pause.*) You don't have one idea what you did. There's nothing sacred to you.

Oberman All right. Now, what is it? What?

Lang You destroyed. You destroyed it.

Oberman What?

Lang You wrecked my lab. (*Pause.*)

Gross Someone wrecked your lab?

Lang I think that I should kill you.

Gross When?

Oberman When was your lab wrecked? (*To* **Gross**) See? You see? I told you.

Lang I don't know. Last night.

Oberman (*to* **Gross**) You see?

Lang You told him what? (*Pause.*)

Oberman You're in great danger, Mr Lang.

Lang You ruined my work.

Oberman 'You' . . . who is that 'You?' You think that Gross and I destroyed your lab?

Lang Yes. You and him.

Oberman We wrecked it. (*To* **Gross**) Do you see? (*Pause.*) Did I tell you?

Oberman and **Gross** *speak simultaneously.*

Gross Yes.

Oberman Why would we do that?

Lang Plans.

Oberman To get your plans.

Lang Yes.

Oberman They stole your plans.

Gross Oh, Christ. (*Pause.*)

Oberman Did they steal your plans!!!?

Lang No.

Oberman No? The plans are safe? (*Pause.*) Are the plans safe?

Lang You people are savages. (*Pause.*) You're animals.

Gross Charles, we did not destroy your lab.

Lang And I came in here to do business with you. We decided to do business.

Gross As God as my Witness. Before God, we did not go . . . why would we do a thing like that? (*Pause.*) Think. *Think.* Why???

Secretary (*on intercom*) Are you in?

Gross No.

Oberman (*interrupting*) One moment: are the plans safe?

Lang Why do you play with me? You know if they're safe or not. (*Pause.*) If they'd stolen them, you wouldn't let me in, you wouldn't let me in, I'd be arrested somewhere, wouldn't I? For some two-dollar wrench I took from Dietz. (*Pause.*)

Oberman They're safe.

Lang Yes. They're safe from you. (*Pause.*) I hid them. You think I'm a fool? I'm not a fool. (*Pause.*)

Oberman They were hidden.

Lang Yeah. You bet they were.

Oberman In the laboratory.

Lang No.

Oberman Where? (*Pause.*)

Lang Somewhere else. (*Pause.*) Should I tell you where?

Oberman The engine, too?

Lang The engine, too. Yes. (*Pause.*)

Oberman So they got nothing.

Lang Oh. Why did you do this, I came to cooperate. I came to do business.

Oberman Who knew?

Lang You.

Oberman Who else?

Lang Just you. You two and my sister.

Oberman Would she tell someone? Who might she tell? (*Pause.*)

Lang Don't you mention her. (*Pause.*)

Gross It might just have been a coincidence. Sometimes . . .

Lang You don't mention her.

Oberman All right. All right. Mr Lang, you're very lucky. You have no idea . . . *business* communities, who knows, that girl out there at the desk, some cab driver, perhaps . . . there are many ways. I think that we are very lucky here. (*Pause.*)

Lang We are lucky. (*Pause.*)

Oberman Yes. Where is the engine?

Lang Hidden.

Oberman Where?

Lang Somewhere safe.

Oberman It must remain safe. I am going to have men assigned. Around you lab and with you, personally. (*He moves to the intercom to do so.*)

Lang You ruined my lab. (*He rises and moves for the door.*)

Gross Where are you going?

Oberman Lang!

Lang Just stay out of my way.

Oberman You can't go out there.

Lang Leave me alone.

Oberman No, you cannot go out there.

Lang Don't threaten me. Don't threaten me. (*Pause.*) You are scum. You're nothing. I'm leaving now, I'm going, maybe I'll come back. If I come back you're going to meet our terms. Our terms. And Oberman? I may go up to your company, I may just say how badly you have botched this up, I make a deal. I go over your head. Part of the deal, you are gone. The both of you. You come in and you destroy my experiments, my work . . . I say I want *all* of the money and we throw you to the wolves. (*Pause.*) Get out of my way.

Gross Charles . . .

Oberman Wait. Now wait . . .

Lang You move aside.

Oberman If you walk out that door now we are going to have to go to Dietz and sue you for possession of the plans. (*Pause.*) You are going to lose.

Lang You do your worst.

Oberman I'm trying to help you.

Lang Get out of my way.

Oberman We'll be here until ten this evening. If you find you need our help.

Lang I don't expect that.

Oberman If you find that you need help.

Lang (*stepping through them.*) Excuse me. (*He leaves the office.*)

Oberman Who said if everyone just acted in his own best interests this would be a paradise on earth. (*He buzzes* **Secretary**.)

Secretary Yes, Sir.

Elevator Operator Down? We're going down . . .

Chain Letter (*voice over*) Make sure you send the letter on to someone who you trust will send the letter on. All people are connected. (*Pause.*) Do not send cash.

Act Two

Lang *is still in the elevator.*

Oberman (*voice over*) Who said that if every man just acted in his own best interests, this would be a paradise on Earth?

Rita They're going to get him now. They're going to get him now. The whole thing will go down. It all goes down when we have given up the things we own.

Announcer (*voice over*) Another chapter, yes, of *Century of Progress!!!*

Rita We must all be careful.

Announcer (*voice over*) You'll remember when we last saw the inventor, Charles Lang, he had just left the offices of Morton Gross.

Elevator Operator Down, we're going down*

Woman (*In elevator*) . . . that people . . . just could die of loneliness.

Companion They could?

Woman This doctor said they could. I read it.

Companion Where?

Woman A magazine.

Companion They must have something else.

Woman What?

Companion A disease.

*The play can be played in one act by proceeding directly from the end of Act One to this line.

Woman No, it said people just could die, you know, if they were lonely.

Companion I don't think so.

Woman Well, I read it.

Companion Where?

Lang *is in the lobby of the office building.*

Elevator Operator Main floor.

Cop Your name Lang?

Lang What?

Cop Is your name Lang? (*Pause.*)

Lang Who are you?

Second Cop This way, please.

Lang Wait, who are you?

They start manhandling **Lang**.

Lang Wait, who are you? Wait. Wait. These men are taking me. Wait.

Cop One side, please.

Lang Who are you?

Cop Stand aside, please, folks, Police.

Lang You're the Police. (*Pause.*) You're the Police?

Second Cop One side, please.

Cop You got him?

Lang You wait here. You don't do this.

Lang *struggles to get free. A fight ensues.* **Lang** *breaks free.*

You won't *do this* . . .

Cop Stop him. Halt! Stop that man.

Second Cop Stop!

Cop Take the back.

Second Cop Stop that man running.

At **Mr Wallace**'s *candy store.*

Mr Wallace And so then, Bernie, on the train they found this man who had been the designer.

Bernie Of the train?

Mr Wallace Yes. Of the train.

Bernie He built it.

Mr Wallace He designed it.

Bernie Uh-huh.

Mr Wallace So they said, they're late, and no one in the crew could fix the engine.

Bernie Yeah.

Mr Wallace They tried and tried.

Bernie Uh-huh.

Mr Wallace And so this man said, 'Let me have a look at it,' he took a light, and looked all at the engine, and he said, 'Give me a hammer.' (*Pause.*) He took the hammer and he found this place, this one place and gave it a little tap, and boom, the engine started right up.
(*Pause.*) Eh? The next week comes a letter for the President of the Railroad, a bill from this man who had fixed the locomotive.

Bernie How much?

Mr Wallace Well, that's what I'm telling you: (*Pause.*) Fifteen thousand dollars.

Bernie No!

Mr Wallace He telephones the man, he says how come you charge me fifteen thousand dollars for one little hammer tap!?

The door opens and **Lang** *enters.*

Bernie Hiya, Mr Lang.

Mr Wallace How *are* you?

Lang Hello.

Mr Wallace We haven't seen you. (*Pause.*) How you doing?

Lang Fine.

Mr Wallace Good. (*Pause.*)

Lang Do you have change for a dollar?

Mr Wallace Sure, Bernie.

Bernie Yes.

Mr Wallace Change for a dollar. You been to the fair since we spoke?

Lang No. I haven't. No.

Bernie *gives him change.*

Thank you. (*He goes to phone.*)

Bernie You're welcome.

Mr Wallace You working hard?

Lang Yes.

Mr Wallace I know. Yep.

Mr Wallace (*to* **Bernie**) Close the register.

Bernie I'm sorry.

Operator The Chicago Daily News.

Lang Hello. I'd like to speak to someone. (*Pause.*)

Operator Who? I'm sorry . . . ?

Lang Someone on the . . . (*Pause.*) City Desk.

Operator Who?

Lang I don't care. The Editor. (*Pause.*) I don't care.

Operator I'm *ringing* . . .

Bernie Pop wants to know if you would like some coffee.

Lang What?

Operator That line is busy.

Lang I'll wait. Thank you. What, I'm sorry. What?

Bernie You want a cup of coffee?

Lang No. Thank you.

Operator I can ring now.

Lang Thank you.

Murray City Desk.

Lang Yes. Who is this?

Murray This is Dave Murray. (*Pause.*) What can I do for you?

Lang You're a reporter?

Murray Yes. What can I do for you?

Lang I'd like to speak with you.

Murray All right. About what? (*Pause.*)

Lang My name is Lang.

Murray L-A-N-G?

Lang I'm an inventor.

Murray Of what?

Lang I, of *things* . . . of *things*. I'm in some trouble.

Murray What kind? (*Pause.*) Are you sure that you don't want the science editor?

Lang Yes. No, please listen to me. I've invented an engine. Some people are stealing my engine.

Murray (*pause*) Uh-huh.

Lang No, these people are trying to take my machine.

Murray Are you all right?

Secretary *places some galleys in front of* **Murray**. *He reads while he talks with* **Lang**.

Lang Please. Oh, please, I swear to you. All the Police are out. They've got them looking for me. Please. I have to talk to you.

Murray *covers mouthpiece. Initials paper.*

Murray (*to* **Secretary**) It's okay. Send it down.

Lang I have to talk to you.

Murray (*into phone*) What? Yeah. All right. All right. Come in.

Lang No. I can't come in.

Murray You say that the cops are after you?

Lang Yes.

Murray For What? (*Long pause.*) All right.

Lang Can you meet me?

Murray Yes.

Lang Thank you.

Murray Nine o'clock.

Lang Before that.

Murray Look, I can't. Unless you come in. (*Pause.*)

Lang The zoo. Can you meet me at the zoo at nine o'clock?

Murray All right.

Lang The zoo. (*Pause.*) God bless you. (*Hangs up phone. Pause.*)

Murray Nine o'clock. Lincoln Park Zoo. (*Sighs.*) Well, a Free Press is the first defense for liberty. Or words to that effect.

Lang *telephones* **Rita**.

Lang Rita?

Rita Yes. Yes. Oh, where are you?

Lang Are you all right?

Rita Yes. Please. Charlie, I'm so worried.

Lang Now, don't worry. Everything is going to be all right. I'm meeting with a man tonight. I'm going to tell the newspapers.

Rita When?

Lang This evening.

Rita Come here now.

Lang I can't.

Rita I'm frightened.

Lang You'll be fine. Just keep the doors and windows locked, and I will come there when I've met with the reporter. (*Pause.*)

Rita Will you be all right?

Lang Yes.

Rita I'm so worried about you Charlie.

Lang We will both be fine. (*Pause.*) I am going to go now, and I'll be there when I've met with him.

Rita Yes.

Lang Everything will be all right. (*Pause.*)

Rita When we are famous.

Lang Yes.

Rita And we are safe.

Lang I have to go now.

Pause. **Lang** *hangs up. We hear a knocking at the apartment door.* **Rita** *does not answer. The knock is repeated.*

Rita (*tentatively*) What? Who is it?

Mrs Varĕc Mrs Varĕc from upstairs.

Rita Oh, good. Oh, thank god.

Mrs Varĕc Can I get you anything?

Rita Wait, Mrs Varĕc . . . (*She goes to and unlocks the door.*)

Mrs Varĕc Can I come in?

Rita Yes. Mrs Varĕc, come in.

In the candy store. **Lang** *hangs up the telephone. The cops are talking to* **Mr Wallace**.

Cop Have you see this man?

Mr Wallace Sure.

Cop When?

Mr Wallace All the time. He lives around here.

Cop He been in here.

Mr Wallace Sure.

Cops When?

Mr Wallace Regularly. He lives in the neighborhood.

Cop He been in today?

Mr Wallace No. (*Pause.*)

Cop Thanks.

Second Cop Call in.

Cop (*to* **Mr Wallace**) Where's your phone?

Mr Wallace It's broken.

Cops *exit.* **Mr Wallace** *stays in front of his store watching cops.*

Stay in the booth there, Mr Lang. They're right across the street and they can see you. They're policemen?

Lang I don't know. (*Pause.*)

Mr Wallace Bernie! Bernie.

Bernie What, Pop?

Mr Wallace Get down here.

Bernie I'm coming.

Mr Wallace He'll take you out the cellar, out the back. (*Pause.*)

Lang Thank you.

Mr Wallace That's all right.

Bernie What, pop?

Mr Wallace You go show Mr Lang the way out through the cellar.

Bernie What's up?

Mr Wallace Just do it.

Bernie Will you be all right?

Lang I'm going to see this man.

Mr Wallace He'll help you?

Lang Yes. I'm seeing him tonight, I'll be all right. I only have to wait 'til then.

Bernie Are you in trouble, Mr Lang?

Mr Wallace (*at window*) My god, they're coming back. (*To* **Bernie**.) Go!! Go!

Bernie C'mon.

They exit. The **Cops** *are circulating. 'Have you seen this man?,' etc.*

At the Hall of Science.

Lecturer Those men all died a violent death. The railroad tycoon, not five months from that day, was stricken with a rare, wasting disease, and died within the year. The match king took his own life, jumping from a building he, himself, had built. The financier died at the hands of gamblers. All these men, that power, in one Hotel Room that night, here in Chicago.

Barker And now we leave The Hall of Science, the hub of our Century of Progress Exposition. Science, yes, the greatest force for Good and Evil we possess. The Concrete Poetry of Humankind. Our thoughts, our dreams, our aspirations rendered into practical and useful forms. Our science is our self. (*Pause.*) What are our tools, but wishes? Much is known and much will *yet* be known, and much will not be known. Those wishing a re-entry to the Hall of half-price, come and get a ticket. This is our last tour tonight.

Everyone mills toward the door. **Lang** *lags behind.*

Barker Closing up. (*Pause.*) Closing up.

Lang I know. Yes. Thank you.

Barker You all right?

Lang What?

Barker Are you all right. I've seen you've been here since this afternoon. (*Pause.*) Are you okay, pal?

Lang Yes.

Barker Sure?

Lang Yes. (*Pause.*)

Barker They're locking up in twenty minutes. (*Pause.*) Come on, I'll walk you to the gate.

Lang What?

Barker Come on. (*Pause.*) Come on, we'll take a walk. (*Pause.*)

Lang Thank you.

Barker I'll punch out.

Lang I have to make a telephone call.

Barker You hold on. I'll be right back. I have to punch out.

Lang What time do you have?

Barker Eight-fifteen.

Barker *exits.* **Lang** *moves to telephone.* **Voice Over** *is the last of a speech from a different pavilion.*

Voice Over Rocket travel, travel to the stars, the wonder of the Universe at last within our grasp. (*Pause.*) Men and women walking on the moon within the lifetime of our children. Who knows *what* they will encounter. By the year two thousand. Travel to the moon and planets. Souvenirs available at the Main Gate. The 'Rocket' ship, the travel of the Future. (*Pause.*) The 'Rocket' Ship.

Lang (*on phone*) Rita?

Mrs Varěc Hello? (*Pause.*)

Lang Who is this?

Mrs Varěc Hello? Who is this? (*Pause.*)

Lang Charles Lang.

Mrs Varěc Charles.

Lang Who am I talking to. Who is this?

Mrs Varěc This is Mrs Varěc.

Lang Mrs Varěc.

Mrs Varěc From upstairs. (*Pause.*)

Lang Where is Rita?

Mrs Varěc You better come over here.

Lang Where is she?

Mrs Varěc Something went on. (*Pause.*)

Lang What?

Mrs Varěc You better call the cops.

Lang What happened?

Mrs Varěc Call the police and they'll tell you.

Lang You tell me. (*Pause.*) *You* tell me.

Mrs Varěc (*pause*) They took her.

Lang They took her.

Mrs Varěc Yeah. (*Pause.*)

Lang Who took her?

Mrs Varěc I don't know.

Lang What happened, for Christ's sake?

Mrs Varěc They came in here.

Lang Who?

Mrs Varěc I don't know. I told them already.

Lang What?

Mrs Varěc I heard these noises.

Lang Yes? Yes? What . . .

Mrs Varěc I heard this screaming. My husband, we came downstairs, the door was broke. (*Pause.*) There was nobody here.

Lang The police came?

Mrs Varěc What?

Lang Did the police come?

Mrs Varěc Yes. They came. They said if you should call

to call them up. A special number. Wait. I'm going to give it to you. (*Hunts.*) Hold on: Lakeview 7-320. (*Pause.*) You better call them. (*Pause.*) Or tell me where you are, they said, and they'll come and get you.

Lang What?

Mrs Varěc They'll come and get you. (*Pause.*) I'm only cleaning up in here.

A long pause. **Lang** *hangs up.*

Mrs Varěc Is that all right?

Unidentified Voice Yes.

Mrs Varěc Will you let me go home now?

Voice Over The Fair is closing. Please proceed to exits on the North and West sides of the Lagoon.

Lang, *again, on the phone.*

Secretary Mr Gross' office . . .

Lang Let me talk to Oberman.

Secretary To *who*, sir?

Lang Let me talk to him. (*Pause.*)

Secretary One moment.

Oberman Hello?

Lang Where is she?

Oberman Good evening.

Lang Where is she? (*Pause.*)

Oberman We can help you find her.

Lang Can you?

Oberman We can find her. (*Pause.*)

Lang Don't hurt her.

Oberman Do you have the plans?

Lang I have them.

Oberman Do you have them with you? (*Pause.*)

Lang I have them.

Oberman Bring them.

Lang Just don't hurt her.

Oberman Now we understand that you had tentatively scheduled an appointment with a journalist this evening.

Lang (*pause*) I won't.

Oberman You see how that would not be in your own best interests.

Lang Yes. (*Pause.*) Let me talk to her.

Oberman One moment. (*Pause.*)

Rita Hello?

Lang Rita?

Rita Charlie!

Lang Are you all right?

Rita What?

Lang Are you *all right*?

Rita I'm all right. Charlie. Yes. I'm all right.

Lang I am going to see you in one hour. I'm going to bring the plans, and then we can go home.

Rita What, *what*? No.

Lang No, you don't understand. When I give them the plans, they're going to let you go. (*Pause.*)

Rita No, I don't think that's a good idea. (*Pause.*)

Lang You don't understand. (*Pause.*) They are going to hurt you if I do not bring them in.

Sounds. **Oberman** *tries to take the phone.*

Rita I understand. Yes. Don't you bring them, Charles. They won't make it. They will just destroy it.

Oberman *wrenches the phone from* **Rita**.

Lang Hello? Hello?

Oberman Where we met last time. In one hour.

Line goes dead. **Lang** *stands alone in the exhibit hall. A pause.*

Voice Over The Fair is Closing . . .

Lang *wanders to an exhibit and reads the placard.*

Lang ' "Lord of the Isles", the celebrated locomotive, attained speeds in excess of one hundred miles an hour before the year 1880 on the broad-guage steel-and-stone way between Bath and London.' (*Pause.*) We could just think ourselves from one place to another. (*Pause.*) she said. Some day. If there is hydrogen and oxygen. If we can free the molecules in Water, Charles . . . we are all made of molecules.

Voice Over *and* **Lang** *speak simultaneously.*

Lang We are all made of light, she said.

Voice Over The Fair is closing.

Lang Machines could extract moisture from the air and fly indefinitely. (*Pause.*)

Voice Over The Fair is closing. Please proceed to exits on the North and West sides of the Lagoon. Lost children can be claimed on the South End of the Architecture Building. The Exhibitors and the Employees of The Century of Progress Exhibition hope that you have had a good day at the Fair, and invite you all to return soon and often.

Barker All done?

Lang What?

Barker Are you done?

Lang (*pause*) Yes.

Barker Come on. I'll walk you to the gate.

They start to walk.

You look glum.

Lang What?

Barker You don't look good.

Lang No. No.

Barker This'll cheer you up. Look what I got in the mail this morning. (*Produces letter and reads*) 'The Ancient Mysteries of Egypt and the East are all within the mind of men.'

Lang What is it?

Barker It's a chain letter.

Voice Over *stops. They stop.* **Barker** *reads:*

'Who knows the real power of man's soul?'
'Much good, much pain and misery is caused by our beliefs.
Great Wealth and Fame stand just beyond your grasp.
All civilization stands on trust.
All people are connected.
No one can call back what one man does.'

Lang What?

Barker I'm sorry?

Lang Would you read that part again? (*Pause.*)

Barker Sure. (*Pause.*) 'All people are connected.'

Lang Yes, yes.

Barker 'No one can call back what one man does.'

Lang Yes, that's right.

Barker (*reading*) 'Much is known and much will *yet* be known and much will not be known.' (*Pause.*) 'Write the names of three friends at the bottom of this list. Send one dollar. . . .' Can you beat this, I'm supposed to send a dollar to three people who I've never heard of. . . . Well, here we are.

Lang Yes. (*Pause.*)

Barker Are you all right?

Lang Yes. I'm all right now.

Barker Did I cheer you up a little?

Lang Yes. You've helped me more than you could know. (*Pause.*)

Barker Well, good night.

Lang Wait. I would like to show you something.

Barker What?

Lang (*produces an envelope containing plans*) These are blueprints.

Barker Well, you'll have to tell me what they mean.

Lang It's an engine.

Barker Uh-huh.

Lang And it uses water for its fuel. I made it. (*Pause.*) I saw it work.

Murray *at his desk at the* Daily News.

Murray The quintessence of those things which made our country great. How much more?

Secretary (*taking dictation*) They need the two columns.

Murray How much more?

Secretary Two hundred words?

Murray All right. (*Pause.*) The Century of Progress, sign and symbol of the great essential strength of the Free

Market. All around the nations founder and decay . . . the East Turns Red, and senile Europe limps from day to day in search of that lost leader, that forgotten vigor never to return. For Europe is the Old Land, and this is the New. The West is Golden with the promise of prosperity to come. The Principles which made this country made it great, as it *is* great, as, once again, it shall be great. With Trust, with power, with a mutual recognizance . . .

Secretary They'll take it out.

Murray With mutual understanding of the simple grace and the eternal power of 'The Bargain Made and Kept To.' Here, now, in Chicago, Phoenix of Communities, we, once again, say, 'I Will,' and rise from the ashes; hardened, strengthened, turned toward the New Day . . . The Day of Progress: The Second Hundred Years of Progress.

Secretary Mmm.

Murray The Century of Progress Exposition enters *its* new life, too, enters on its second year. Let us continue to support it. Thirty.

Secretary Brilliant.

Murray Thank God I don't have to sign it. What have I got on this evening?

Secretary Meeting with that . . .

Murray Right. Right. Mr Lang. 'They stole my engine.'

Secretary That's it.

Murray Meet me afterward?

Secretary Maybe.

Murray Eleven.

Secretary Maybe.

Murray (*after her*) I'll call you.

Bughouse Square

Speaker What happened to this nation? Or did it ever exist? . . . did it exist with its freedoms and slogan . . . the buntings, the gold-headed standards, the songs. With Equality, Liberty . . . In the West they plow under wheat. Where is America? I say it does not exist. And I say that it never existed. It was all but a myth. A great dream of avarice . . . The dream of a Gentleman Farmer.

Lang *at the meeting place with* **Oberman**.

Oberman Where are the plans?

Lang Where is my sister?

Speaker And I say that we live in the Final Time.

Lang My sister is not here?

Oberman You come with me.

Speaker With want in the midst of abundance.

Lang Oh. You'll take me to her.

Oberman Yes.

Speaker As they turn to War in Old Europe, and we live in Fear at Home . . .

Lang When I give you the plans?

Oberman Yes.

Speaker In the final moments. When we, when America irrevocably ceases to be Europe, and commences the fulfillment of its malevolent destiny as The New World.

Oberman Where are the plans?

Lang I'm going to tell you. (*Whispers to* **Oberman**.)

Moderator Anybody else who wants to talk? Does anybody want to speak? (*Pause.*) Anybody want to speak?

Oberman You *what?*

Lang　I put them in the mailbox, Mr Oberman.

Oberman　You *what*?

Lang　You heard me.

Oberman　Do you know what you have done?

Lang　Yes.

Oberman　Do you know that we are going to *find* them?

Lang　No. You'll never find them.

Oberman　Oh, yes. Mr Lang, we will. For you will tell us where they are. Believe me. You will tell us where they are.

Lang　No. I think you will find that that is not the truth.

Moderator　Anybody want to speak? Does anybody want to speak?

At **Mr Wallace**'s *candy store*.

Bernie　Some more coffee?

Customer　Thank you.

Bernie　So where was I? Oh, yes. So a letter comes . . .

Customer　Yeah . . .

Bernie　For the man who owns the railroad.

Customer　Uh-huh.

Bernie　It's a bill, for fifteen thousand dollars.

Customer　No.

Bernie　Yeah. So he calls the guy up . . .

Mr Wallace　My boy taking care of you, M'am?

Customer　Yes, Mr Wallace.

Mr Wallace　Good boy. Good.

Bernie And so he calls the guy and asks him, 'How come fifteen thousand dollars for one hammer tap . . . ?'

Customer Yeah.

Bernie And so the guys say, 'I gave you the hammer tap for nothing, and the fifteen thousand dollars . . .'

Customer Yeah.

Bernie 'The fifteen thousand dollars was for *knowing where to tap.*' (*Pause.*) Huh?

Customer Yeah.

Bernie For *knowing where to tap.* (*Pause.*)

Customer *Yeah.* Ah *ha* . . . ! (*Gets up to leave. Hands* **Bernie** *a coin.*)

Bernie Thank you.

Customer Mr Wallace . . .

Mr Wallace Yeah.

Customer You have a good boy here.

Mr Wallace I know it. Have a nice day.
(**Customer** *exits.*)

Murray *phones in to the* Daily News.

Operator *Daily News* . . .

Murray Gimme rewrite.

Operator What?

Murray Rewrite.

Operator One moment, please.

Rewrite Rewrite.

Murray Ernie?

Rewrite Yeah?

Murray Dave Murray.

Rewrite How are you?

Murray Fine. Ready?

Rewrite Shoot.

Murray Waukegan, Illinois, David M. Murray, Special to the *Daily News* today's date, 7:30, make it 6:30 a.m. The mutilated bodies of a man and woman were discovered in the early morning hours on a stretch of industrial lake frontage five miles north of Waukegan today, period.

The man and woman both were white and in their early thirties, period.

The cause of death in both cases appears to have been drowning, comma, but both bodies bear signs of quite extensive injury, period. The Illinois State Police and the Lake County Sheriff's Office are conducting a fullscale inquiry, comma, and an autopsy later in the day should establish positively the cause or causes of death. Period. That's it.

Rewrite Got it.

Murray Tell the lab they got a picture they can get off the State Cops for the late edition.

Rewrite Right.

Murray It isn't pretty. Can you buzz upstairs?

Rewrite Sure. (*Buzzes.*)

Secretary City Desk.

Murray How are you?

Secretary Where the hell have you been?

Murray Did you miss me?

Secretary I've been waiting since eleven.

Murray Yeah, I'm sorry, but I just got done.

Secretary Where are you?

Murray In Waukegan.

Secretary I thought that you were going to the zoo, for God's sake.

Murray Yeah, 'they took my engine.' Well he stood me up, I'm up here on these drowning deaths.

Secretary Will you be back today?

Murray I think so. Yeah. I'll call you.

Secretary Will you?

Murray Yeah.

Secretary Good. (*They hang up.*)

At the candy store.

Mr Wallace Bernie.

Bernie What?

Mr Wallace What did you do? (*Pause.*)

Bernie What? (*Pause.*)

Mr Wallace What did you do?

Bernie I left the drawer open. (*Pause.*) I'm sorry.

Mr Wallace You cannot leave the drawer open in the day. (*Pause.*)

Bernie I'm sorry.

Mr Wallace Do you want that chemistry set?

Bernie Yes.

Mr Wallace All right then.

A paperboy drops off a bundle of papers.

Paperboy Papers.

Bernie *puts the papers up on the counter.*

Mr Wallace Thank you. (*Looks at papers.*) Oh, my god.

Bernie What?

Mr Wallace Oh my god.

Bernie What is it, Pop?

Mr Wallace I can't believe this. (*Pause.*)

Bernie What *is* it?

Mr Wallace Sit down. I am going to read you this. (*Pause.*) 'Free day at the Exposition. Monday, Wednesday, Friday afternoons to anybody under twelve when accompanied by an adult.'

Bernie *cheers.*

Do you want to go?

Bernie Yes!

Mr Wallace Then watch the cash.

Mailman Mailman!

Mr Wallace And what have you got for us today?

Mailman *hands letters.*

Mailman (*to* **Bernie**) And it seems I've got one for you.

Hands **Bernie** *a letter which* **Bernie** *opens and reads during the following speech. The letter contains the plans of the Water Engine.*

Barker And so we leave the Hall of Science, the Hub of our Century of Progress Exposition. Science, yes, the greatest force for Good and Evil we possess. The concrete Poetry of Humankind. (*Pause.*) Much is known and much will *yet* be known, and much will not be known. As we complete our second thousand years. In the dilapidated office buildings, and in rooms in Railroad Hotels, in torn and filthy manuscripts misfiled in second-hand bookstores, here rest the vestiges of this and other cultures. Arcane Knowledge in transition from the inaccessible to the occult, as we rush on. (*Pause.*)

Technological and Ethic masterpieces decay into folktales. Who knows what is true? All people are connected.

Chain Letter (*voice over*) One man saw the plans for a machine which he was told would run on water as its only fuel. A woman in Tacoma received seven thousand dollars, but she lost her life because she broke the chain.

Bernie Hey, Pop.

Mr Wallace What?

Bernie Look what I got in the mail.

Barker The Fair is closing. Those who wish re-entry to the Hall at half-price, see me for a ticket. This is our last tour tonight. They're good tomorrow, though.

Mr Happiness

Mr Happiness was first produced at the Plymouth Theatre on Broadway on March 6, 1978, New York City, with Charles Kimbrough as Mr Happiness. The production was directed by Steven Schachter; set by John Lee Beatty; lighting by Dennis Parichy; original music composed by Alaric Jans; produced by Joseph Papp; associated producer, Bernard Gersten.

Mr Happiness is set in a radio station studio in 1934.

Mr Happiness *is seated at a desk behind an old-fashioned microphone.*

Mr Happiness One listener writes:
'Dear Mr Happiness:

I am thirty-five years old, unmarried. I live with my mother. Mr Happiness, she is a burden on me. I am not unattractive, I've been told, and I've had men friends. I was engaged once in the War, but he died. So I am no stranger to the ways of Love, if you will think back to that period. I am no stranger to wanting and the need of *care*. But, Mr Happiness, my mother is an invalid who lays around the house; and I have "done" for her for six years now. Since she left Bill, my brother's, in New Haven to come live with me.

The time has come for me to leave. I have been seeing this man who I met at work, and last week he asked me to marry him.

I said "yes," please believe me, very quickly. "What about my mother, though?" I asked.

He said he thought she could come live with us, but I know that he only said that because he thought that's what I would like to hear. *I* do not want my mother living with us.

I am sick and tired of her ways – for lately she has become very grouchy.

Do you think it would be "alright" if I told her I am moving out and my new husband just won't hear of her coming to live with us so she had better go back to New Haven? (*Pause.*) 'What do you think? As this is almost true.

Also:

How can my marriage after all these years be possibly considered as unfaithfulness to my late fiancé, who gave his life that we may live.

Awaiting your reply,
"I've Got some Good Years Left" '

Hmmm.

Dear 'I've Got Some Good Years':

And I'll say you do, and no mistake. Here's what I say:

Down through the ages it has been a battle inside of the Race and inside every one of us to balance selflessness and Greed. And it's still going on.

Of *course* you have some good years left in you.

They *all* are good years when they're balanced. (*Beat.*)

The mouth says 'take,' the hands say 'take' – what does the heart say? '*Give.*' That's right. 'Give.'

And, Dear, here's where the *Head* comes in. What do we always say? 'Follow the dictates of your Heart, but Use your Head.' And keep your Two Eyes Open. Dear, it's such sage advice, and it doesn't originate here. I just echo it. (*Pause.*) And you know it yourself. Alright. (*Pause.*)

Now your mother. She needs somewhere to go. She is unwell. She cannot live alone.

Your brother had her, but six years ago she came to live with you. We know not why. If he were prone to take her voluntarily back you wouldn't take the time to write to *me*. I wouldn't now be *speaking* to you. Fine.

Your husband says that he would take her in. You find this unacceptable. Fine. Your Mother. What does she want? Let's assume she wants to stay right where she is.

She's old. She is an invalid. Although I *think* you give us to suspect that she is shamming. (*Pause.*) If only partially.

We *all* know how infuriating that can be. I'm sure if we could crack the secrets of the unsolved crimes of ages *many*, *many* would be founded on *exactly* situations like your own.

Alright.

Mom wants to stay, you want her out. Your hubby doesn't *like* the prospect, no. But he's prepared to put her up if you so wish. Your *brother* doesn't want her. (*Pause.*)

I think the *answer* here is 'Put her in a Home.'

And all you regulars know that I say that seldom. *Seldom.*

Have your husband . . . (I think . . . yes.) *approach* your brother on a friendly basis, yes, but not unmindful of the six years you've relieved him of his rightful burden – and *request* that he contribute to her upkeep in the institution.

Now: he may have been sending her money while she lived with *you*. (*Beat.*) We don't *know*. You didn't *tell* us.

Also: in addition to or, if it should *eventuate*, in *place* of monies from your brother, ask your *husband*.

Ask him. What is it we say?

'You never know until you *ask*.'

'The worst thing that can happen is they will say "NO." '

That is the worst.

You never know until you ask.

Ask hubby to contribute to her maintenance. Between the two of them I'm certain some arrangement can be made to keep her safe, and comfortable, and *cared*-for. In her final years.

Don't be embarrassed. Face the facts. The facts may be *unpleasant*, but they always are the facts.

You *want*, and you deserve to live. (*Beat.*) Live! (*Beat.*) Live.

Think of your warrior fiancé, your fallen fiancé with reverence. Don't forget him, no. He gave his life for you.

But do not *dote* on him. (*Pause.*)

He is dead.

Your sentiments are noble, but they are misplaced.

Keep your respectful memories for him, and give that long lost love to your *new* husband.

Good Luck, and God Bless You,

Mr Happiness

Alright. Remember, Friends. (*Beat.*) If it were not *one* thing, it would *surely* be another.

What's important? (*Beat.*) Your *attitude!*

That's right.

Let's move along.

'Dear Mr Happiness:

I'm married to a woman who I do not Love.'

Beat.

Love. Everyone's talking about Love.

You know, I say it every week, and I'll say it again. The situations that I see – *your* troubles . . . (they're my troubles too) . . .

They had them back in Bible Times (They did. Oh, yes. They did. Just read your Bible), and they'll have them in the future when we . . . *I* don't know . . . we live in *air*, or whatever the Master has in store for us. (*Beat.*)

People do not change.

'Dear Mr Happiness:

'I'm married to a woman who I do not love. I'm forty-one and she is thirty-five. I'm a policeman, and I have four children ranged in age from two to thirteen years. I love them very much . . .'

There is the story. *There's* the rub. We do not *act*ually have to read another word. (*Beat.*) *Do* we?

Mr Happiness *sighs. Beat.*

'. . . ranged in age from two to thirteen, and I love them very much.

Our home has been a solid one, and no one in our house has ever wanted. (*Beat.*) Or gone without.

Nor will they, come what may. . . .'

Ah. These are Noble Sentiments. (*Beat.*) '. . . come what may. But I have met a woman. Eighteen months ago in the performance of my job, and she and I are deeply in love with each other.' (*Sighs.*) 'I want to leave my wife. I know that this will break her and the children's heart.

But I can't live a lie. What can I do?'

And it's signed 'Just a Man.'

Well, 'Just a Man.' I'm going to tell you.

Everything is true if you believe it.

You're a *Police* officer. And in your line of work – and may god *Bless* you for it, it's a thankless job – you see a lot of men.

A fellow with a smoking gun is standing over the proprietor of some poor candy store.

'I had to do it. I don't know. I was just *driven* to it.

(*Beat.*) I didn't mean to kill him, but I had to have the money.' (*Beat.*) He *had* to do it, he tells you. He had no choice. The owner's poor wife in the background, what must she think? Her husband's slayer tells her that he 'had to do it,' and he meant no harm.

But will he stay and stack the shelves, and pay the monthly bills and marshal the accounts?

And will he raise her children? (*Pause.*)

He 'had to do it' . . .

Officer, I'm sure that you see *many* things in your job. During the performance of your duty.

Some young woman hired as a steno fresh from school. She's working at the bank. *Deeply* in love.

Young and in love.

Her lover yearns for things. A new coat. (*Beat.*)

An evening on the *town* . . . an *auto* . . .

Everybody *else*, it seems, is comfortable. Happy. Free from want.

The rich live off the poor and live in *luxury*.

They've taken it from *us*. (*Beat.*) Why not take a little back? A small amount. A hundred dollars.

They will never miss it.

How he reasons with her. 'You will not be caught.'

'Please. If you love me.'

Oh, she loves him, Officer. We know that very well.

But you have caught her with her fingers in the till. (*Beat.*) She was trusted and she vowed not to betray that trust. And there she stands, 'I had to do it. Please! I could not *help* myself. I love him. (*Beat.*) I could not *help* myself.'

But she's broken the *law*..

She's betrayed those to whom she swore allegiance.

And, Officer . . . and I don't care if you don't *ever* like it . . . *you've* taken an oath.

You took (and you may call me 'old-fashioned,' if you will. I *am* old-fashined. I am *proud* of it.) – you took an oath. To be true to your wife. To care for her and raise your family.

Not 'Sometime.'

Not 'While it was *comfortable*.' No. But *all* the time.

All of the time.

You say you are in love, but how can love thrive on deceit?

You know that it cannot. You know that only misery can flourish in deceit.

Do not defile your home.

Do not betray those who love you.

We know how you long. We none of us are strangers to temptation.

But . . . do *not* give in.

You are a man. You have the power to say 'no.' (*Beat.*) *Say* no.

Look your wife and children in the eye, and *build* with them.

Do not defile you home. (*Pause.*) Please (*Pause.*)

   Mr Happiness

Confidential to P.G. in Fairfield:

See a doctor. I am neither fit nor qualified to respond to this inquiry. (*Beat.*) See a doctor. And, as you know, all correspondence sent to me is *absolutely* confidential.

Absolutely. It is *seen* by no one but myself.

My files are locked and are *available* to no one but myself.

'I've told you, Friends, that I've been asked before . . . that I have received *telegrams* and *personal* visits pleading with me to divulge a name. (*Pause.*)

I have received threats.

But let me say it once again and simply: (*Beat.*)

All correspondence sent to me is *absolutely* confidential. *Absolutely.* (*Pause.*)

A young man writes: 'Dear Mr Happiness:

I am a boy of fifteen, and afflicted with a small, but noticeable misalignment of my spine which causes me to limp. When I was young . . .'

Hmm. I suppose everything's relative . . .

'. . . when I was young it was . . .'

What is this?

'. . . painful. But through therapy I learned to overcome the pain.

I read a lot, as I cannot play baseball, or dance very well. Although I'm not sure anyone would dance with me if I *could* dance.'

Mr Happiness *reads a while to himself, mumbling.*

I'm going to skip the next part here. (*Reads to himself.*) 'The Junior *prom* . . .' (*Beat.*) His problem is how should he ask her to the Junior Prom. (*Continues reading.*) '. . . the *prom* . . . and *advice* that you might give . . . ashamed to speak to my *father* . . .' Boy. I'm going to stop right here. You *speak* to your father. Your father is *proud* of you. I swear he is.

Do you know why he's proud of you.

Because he *knows* you. Cause he knows how *brave* you are.

And this 'Miss X' you mention?

People are not *mind* readers!

It's difficult to *tell* what is in someone else's heart.

The kind of person that someone is.

I'm going to tell you something, son: Miss X?

Now when she looks at you you *think* she shies away.

Well, boy, it's up to you to take the helm.

This woman does not know what's in your heart.

She cannot read your mind!

And when – let's put our cards up on the table here.

Let's not mince words.

When Miss X looks at you she does not see a boy who *limps*, she sees a boy who *waivers*, son. Who vacillates.

People will accept you on the selfsame terms that you accept yourself.

Talk to your father.

I'm sure he is full of pride for you. For your work.

For your reading and achievement.

You have overcome your pain. That was a monumental task.

I know it was. I'm *sure* it was.

The only demon that you have to face right now is *bashfulness*.

And I never met a girl who wasn't charmed by bashfulness.

Charmed. But not won.

Assert yourself. There's nothing deep here. *Ask* her. (*Pause.*)

And have a great time at the Prom.

Yours,

Mr Happiness (*Beat.*)

P.S.: Drop me a line and tell me if she let you pin her corsage on. (*Pause.*)

Oh. It takes *time*. It all takes *time*.

You know it's been eight years, now. (*Beat.*)

My *golly* how they do go by!

And I'd bet I could count the different problems that you write me of – and *thank* you, folks, for trusting me. For turning to me with your troubles . . .

I'd bet I could count the different problems that you speak of in, say, thirty thousand letters I've received – *I* don't know. (*Beat.*) It could be twice that number – on the fingers of one hand.

We Need. We Love. We love too much. We love too little . . .

And maybe the most frequent one:

We just do not know who to turn to. (*Beat.*)

We need a friend. (*Beat.*)

Folks, you know that I'm no doctor. I'm no priest.

I'm no professor. Many times I'm *wrong*.

Often I'm wrong.

But in those times when advice I might give – it's only simple common sense – may serve to help you out, you may sit back and say, 'My Golly! You know, it all seems so *simple* now. What makes that man so smart?'

Well, folks, I'm going to tell you.

And it's not intelligence. It isn't even insight. (*Pause.*)

It's *distance*.

The ability to see the facts without becoming side-
tracked by the *history*.

By – and I know they're painful and they're meaningful
– *particulars*. (*Beat*.)

Who said what to whom, and who forgot the birthday.

Yes, it's *distance*, Friends.

And when I tell you that in all the letters that I get the
most, the *most* recurrent problem is just this. It boils down
to this: We don't know where to *turn*. We feel *alone*. We
need a friendly ear to tell our troubles to. . . .

Well, when I say that it sounds hackneyed. It sounds
simple. But it's true.

Someone to say, 'Why, I did the same thing *myself*,
when I was your age.' Or 'Just wait it out.'

Where can we turn? *Where* are our friends?

Who would listen to our woes?

Just look around you. (*Beat*.) Believe me.

Oh. You say, 'I couldn't just *presume* on someone!'
(*Beat*.) 'I couldn't just *intrude*! What would they *think?!*'
'No. I could never do that.'

But just stop and think a second.

Those same folks you say that you could never talk to.

If they came to you and said, 'I have a *problem*, and I
wonder if we just could *talk* about it for a moment.'

Why, how would you feel? (*Pause*.)

Wouldn't you be glad to help them out?

And you would probably be flattered that they *asked*
you. (*Beat*.) Now *wouldn't* you? (*Beat*.) *Well* then! (*Beat*.)
What makes you think that they'd feel any different if you
asked *them?* (*Pause*.) We all need a friend, folks, we all
need somebody to just tell our troubles to. (*Beat*.)
Somebody with *distance*.

We all need a friend.

Confidential to M.P.D.:

Yes. Absolutely. And no one need ever know.

Don't kid yourself. They'd do the same to you.

Confidential to A.B. in Springfield:
  Just read the letter that you wrote to *me* to *him*.
  I've sent it back to you and it should be arriving later in the week.
  God bless you.

Takes new letter.

Oh yes. (*Beat.*)
  No. I think that we'll do this one next week. (*Pause.*) This one can afford to wait a week.

Confidential to 'Mistreated':
  I don't want to *hear* about it.
  Take a good *look* at yourself. (*Pause.*)

Friends, I've received quite a number of requests for 'Twenty-Four Hours a Day' from those of you who couldn't find it in your local bookstores.
  If you'll write to me at:
          Box 'K'
          Chelsea Station
          New York, New York, Zone Eleven
and enclose a postal order for Two Dollars, Fifty Cents
. . . that's two dollars for the book and fifty cents for handling and postage, we will send it out to you.
  Remember to include your name and your return address, or else we won't know who to send it *to*.
  God Bless you all. It's a great honor and a privilege to spend this time with you. (*Beat.*) And remember:
  If you want to *have* a friend (*Beat.*) *be* a friend.
  Until next week, then, I remain,
    Sincerely yours, (*Beat.*)
    Mr Happiness.

Methuen Drama Contemporary Dramatists

include

John Arden (two volumes)
Arden & D'Arcy
Peter Barnes (three volumes)
Sebastian Barry
Dermot Bolger
Edward Bond (eight volumes)
Howard Brenton
 (two volumes)
Richard Cameron
Jim Cartwright
Caryl Churchill (two volumes)
Sarah Daniels (two volumes)
Nick Darke
David Edgar (three volumes)
David Eldridge
Ben Elton
Dario Fo (two volumes)
Michael Frayn (three volumes)
David Greig
John Godber (two volumes)
Paul Godfrey
John Guare
Lee Hall (two volumes)
Peter Handke
Jonathan Harvey
 (two volumes)
Declan Hughes
Terry Johnson (two volumes)
Sarah Kane
Barrie Keefe
Bernard-Marie Koltès
David Lan
Bryony Lavery
Deborah Levy
Doug Lucie
David Mamet (four volumes)

Martin McDonagh
Duncan McLean
Anthony Minghella
 (two volumes)
Tom Murphy (five volumes)
Phyllis Nagy
Anthony Nielsen
Philip Osment
Gary Owen
Louise Page
Stewart Parker (two volumes)
Joe Penhall
Stephen Poliakoff
 (three volumes)
David Rabe
Mark Ravenhill
Christina Reid
Philip Ridley
Willy Russell
Eric-Emmanuel Schmitt
Ntozake Shange
Sam Shepard (two volumes)
Simon Stephens
Shelagh Stephenson
Wole Soyinka (two volumes)
David Storey (three volumes)
Sue Townsend
Judy Upton
Michel Vinaver
 (two volumes)
Arnold Wesker (two volumes)
Michael Wilcox
Roy Williams
Snoo Wilson (two volumes)
David Wood (two volumes)
Victoria Wood

Methuen Drama World Classics

include

Jean Anouilh (two volumes)
Brendan Behan
Aphra Behn
Bertolt Brecht (eight volumes)
Büchner
Bulgakov
Calderón
Čapek
Anton Chekhov
Noël Coward (eight volumes)
Feydeau
Eduardo De Filippo
Max Frisch
John Galsworthy
Gogol
Gorky (two volumes)
Harley Granville Barker
  (two volumes)
Victor Hugo
Henrik Ibsen (six volumes)
Jarry

Lorca (three volumes)
Marivaux
Mustapha Matura
David Mercer (two volumes)
Arthur Miller (five volumes)
Molière
Musset
Peter Nichols (two volumes)
Joe Orton
A. W. Pinero
Luigi Pirandello
Terence Rattigan
  (two volumes)
W. Somerset Maugham
  (two volumes)
August Strindberg
  (three volumes)
J. M. Synge
Ramón del Valle-Inclán
Frank Wedekind
Oscar Wilde

Methuen Drama Modern Plays

include work by

Edward Albee
Jean Anouilh
John Arden
Margaretta D'Arcy
Peter Barnes
Sebastian Barry
Brendan Behan
Dermot Bolger
Edward Bond
Bertolt Brecht
Howard Brenton
Anthony Burgess
Simon Burke
Jim Cartwright
Caryl Churchill
Noël Coward
Lucinda Coxon
Sarah Daniels
Nick Darke
Nick Dear
Shelagh Delaney
David Edgar
David Eldridge
Dario Fo
Michael Frayn
John Godber
Paul Godfrey
David Greig
John Guare
Peter Handke
David Harrower
Jonathan Harvey
Iain Heggie
Declan Hughes
Terry Johnson
Sarah Kane
Charlotte Keatley
Barrie Keeffe
Howard Korder

Robert Lepage
Doug Lucie
Martin McDonagh
John McGrath
Terrence McNally
David Mamet
Patrick Marber
Arthur Miller
Mtwa, Ngema & Simon
Tom Murphy
Phyllis Nagy
Peter Nichols
Sean O'Brien
Joseph O'Connor
Joe Orton
Louise Page
Joe Penhall
Luigi Pirandello
Stephen Poliakoff
Franca Rame
Mark Ravenhill
Philip Ridley
Reginald Rose
Willy Russell
Jean-Paul Sartre
Sam Shepard
Wole Soyinka
Shelagh Stephenson
Peter Straughan
C. P. Taylor
Theatre de Complicite
Theatre Workshop
Sue Townsend
Judy Upton
Timberlake Wertenbaker
Roy Williams
Snoo Wilson
Victoria Wood

Methuen Drama Classical Greek Dramatists

Aeschylus Plays: One
(Persians, Seven Against Thebes, Suppliants,
Prometheus Bound)

Aeschylus Plays: Two
(Oresteia: Agamemnon, Libation-Bearers, Eumenides)

Aristophanes Plays: One
(Acharnians, Knights, Peace, Lysistrata)

Aristophanes Plays: Two
(Wasps, Clouds, Birds, Festival Time, Frogs)

Aristophanes & Menander: New Comedy
(Women in Power, Wealth, The Malcontent,
The Woman from Samos)

Euripides Plays: One
(Medea, The Phoenician Women, Bacchae)

Euripides Plays: Two
(Hecuba, The Women of Troy, Iphigeneia at Aulis,
Cyclops)

Euripides Plays: Three
(Alkestis, Helen, Ion)

Euripides Plays: Four
(Elektra, Orestes, Iphigenia in Tauris)

Euripides Plays: Five
(Andromache, Herakles' Children, Herakles)

Euripides Plays: Six
(Hippolytos, Suppliants, Rhesos)

Sophocles Plays: One
(Oedipus the King, Oedipus at Colonus, Antigone)

Sophocles Plays: Two
(Ajax, Women of Trachis, Electra, Philoctetes)

Methuen Drama Student Editions

Jean Anouilh *Antigone* • John Arden *Serjeant Musgrave's Dance* • Alan Ayckbourn *Confusions* • Aphra Behn *The Rover* • Edward Bond *Lear* • Bertolt Brecht *The Caucasian Chalk Circle* • *Life of Galileo* • *Mother Courage and her Children* • *The Resistible Rise of Arturo Ui* • *The Threepenny Opera* • Anton Chekhov *The Cherry Orchard* • *The Seagull* • *Three Sisters* • *Uncle Vanya* • Caryl Churchill *Serious Money* • *Top Girls* • Shelagh Delaney *A Taste of Honey* • Euripides *Elektra* • *Medea* • Dario Fo *Accidental Death of an Anarchist* • Michael Frayn *Copenhagen* • John Galsworthy *Strife* • Nikolai Gogol *The Government Inspector* • Robert Holman *Across Oka* • Henrik Ibsen *A Doll's House* • *Hedda Gabler* • Charlotte Keatley *My Mother Said I Never Should* • Bernard Kops *Dreams of Anne Frank* • Federico García Lorca *Blood Wedding* • *The House of Bernarda Alba* (bilingual edition) • *Yerma* (bilingual edition) • David Mamet *Glengarry Glen Ross* • *Oleanna* • Patrick Marber *Closer* • Joe Orton *Loot* • Luigi Pirandello *Six Characters in Search of an Author* • Mark Ravenhill *Shopping and F***ing* • Willy Russell *Blood Brothers* • Sophocles *Antigone* • Wole Soyinka *Death and the King's Horseman* • August Strindberg *Miss Julie* • J. M. Synge *The Playboy of the Western World* • Theatre Workshop *Oh What a Lovely War* • Timberlake Wertenbaker *Our Country's Good* • Arnold Wesker *The Merchant* • Oscar Wilde *The Importance of Being Earnest* • Tennessee Williams *A Streetcar Named Desire* • *The Glass Menagerie* • Timberlake Wertenbaker *Our Country's Good*

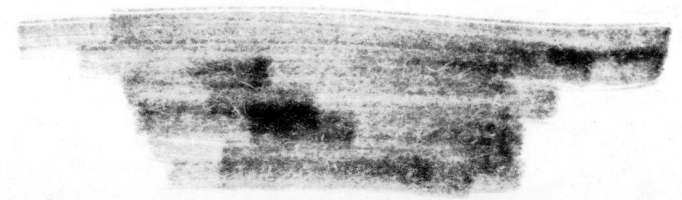

For a complete catalogue of Methuen Drama titles
write to:

Methuen Drama
A & C Black Publishers Limited
38 Soho Square
London
W1D 3HB

or you can visit our website at:

www.acblack.com